THE SHATTERED RING

THE SHATTERED RING

science fiction
and the quest for meaning

LOIS
and
STEPHEN
ROSE

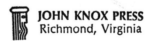

JOHN KNOX PRESS
Richmond, Virginia

Standard Book Number: 8042-1967-2
Library of Congress Catalog Card Number: 70-103465
© M. E. Bratcher 1970
Printed in the United States of America

for
Jim Mason
and
Jack Brennan —
wanderers and wisemen

preface

One day in 1967 I wrote a column in which I said that science fiction—with its emphasis on imaginary post-holocaust worlds—contained a suggestion that the Papacy might be one of the few Christian institutions to survive in the long run. (I had been reading James Blish's delightful science fiction exploration of good and evil, *A Case of Conscience*, in which—on papal instruction—a far-off planet populated by unfallen creatures is "exorcized.")

A few weeks after the column appeared, the editor of *Enquiry*, Wilbur Patterson, asked if I might do an article on science fiction and theology. My immediate response was no, but my wife, Lois, a long-time mythology and science fiction buff and the philosopher of the household, could. Could we do the article together? The answer was yes, and out of the series of odd and happy coincidences comes . . . this study.

What emerged was a happening of sorts, for we found in science fiction a companion in a dialogue about what might precede an effective stance in today's world. We found ourselves writing a prologue to a theology of freedom.

Theology is inevitably a child of its age. As such it is tied to the world view of the time, the issues which are uppermost in the minds of people and the historical events which confront us and, to some extent, determine our actions. This is not to say that there is no continuity in the making of theology. There are certain recurring themes from the earliest pre–Old Testament writers onward, questions about the meaning of man, nature, and history. But the interpretation of these themes and the language with which they are dealt must continually change. Issues may loom large in a particular historical period which lend a distortion to any "system" of interpretation or body of speculation, but, as Kierkegaard has pointed out, these distortions may be a needed vehicle for the truth at the time.

Art helps man to define the theological questions of a given era, and also carries within it seeds of response to the quest for meaning. But art today seems to cry chaos, meaninglessness. We are to take what meaning we can from the moment. However, living for the moment without interpretation has limits, and it may be necessary to turn from nihilistic or totally sensual art to what has been traditionally called "folk art" to isolate questions and some beginnings of a useful world view.

As we prepared this manuscript, many of the idols that stood behind much of society came crashing down. The trauma of assassinations blurred into the madnesses of Biafra and the ABM. An end, if not *the* end, was at hand. The study of science fiction became for us a means of sorting things out, of entering the first phase of an exploration called for by the French thinker Jacques Ellul. Ellul had written—between the political traumas of 1968 and the university chaos of 1969—words that seemed the only hopeful suggestion Christian philosophy might make to modern industrial man:

> Only total and true freedom will make possible the discovery of a new style of life. Yet man will not

find that freedom in himself. . . . But behold, the good news of the gospel affirms precisely that in Christ and through Christ we are free (provided that we live the faith!). "It is for freedom that Christ has set you free." . . . But . . . if the freedom which is given us is to exist, we must live it, desire it and utilize it. . . .

Finally, to attempt such an undertaking—to construct a new morality, a new justice, a new peace and authentic new human relations . . . —needs not only hope and freedom but power of a kind that is certainly beyond human possibilities. . . . It is the power of the Holy Spirit that can make that revolution.[1]

"Endings to be useful must be inconclusive,"[2] says Samuel Delany, the young author whose work constitutes the final direction of this study. It may be, however, that the combining of the classic attitude of folktales (man's use of his wits and courage to triumph) and myths (man's perception of destiny in story) found in some science fiction is a hopeful sign—pointing not to the ghastly worlds projected by Aldous Huxley and George Orwell, or the ineffective voluntarism of H. G. Wells, but to a move beyond the political, economic, and religious despair of the present.

—Stephen C. Rose
Stockbridge
Epiphany, 1970

contents

SCIENCE FICTION —
what is it?

1

If a remnant survives us and looks back centuries hence, our era may be marked as the Time of Explosion when everything was up for grabs, including the very definition of man himself. . . . When the media exploded conscience into a new social consciousness. When the fission bombs produced the first man-made mutations. When forms and structures of centuries' standing cracked, eroded at the foundation by . . . well, in the 1960's one was not sure whether the present order would be brought down by a shot of new wine or a tidal wave, by some computer-imposed grid for the reformulation of life or a revolt against computers so powerful that a period of anarchy, chaos, and totalitarian reaction would be the certain result. Or something unguessed.

"We needed," mused the young Jacob Brackman speaking of his generation, "we needed new definitions of livelihood, of maturity and enjoyment, but we could scarcely imagine a change so gargantuan it seemed close to reversal, so inaccessible to legislation or 'programs' as to demand a radicalism of messianic proportions . . . Great numbers began to conceive of something more decent than submitting to the culture. There was that vague and fragile chance, and although I had great contempt for much my generation spawned, I could not see another chance anywhere I looked."[1]

As the 1960's expired, with their memory of assassination, mass frustration, countless sadnesses wracking the rich spirit-starved body of America–England–France–West Germany (core of the wealthy White West), one learned that, in the walled world of man's self-created box, there had to be some move beyond that impotent psychic state of vacillation between tentative optimism and new pessimism with every turn of the newsprint page. One knew, too, the environmental judgment already close to enactment: that whether or not man began to love or help the poor, the world was on the verge of suffocation, overpopulation—as witnessed by the strangling of the city with its greenish haze of poisoned air and the drawn-out death of infants in one thousand daily unrecorded repeats of Biafran foodlessness.

God gave Adam and Eve garments to wear when they were thrust beyond the gates of Eden. Would the tired white Western specimen of man—man without heroes, without a redeeming mythology, for years without fiction, up-tight with science—would he or, pray God, his children be given proper garments for life in the land of paper dresses, plastic boots, and the telltale cry?

Science fiction had pointed to the present crisis almost casually, before most could see. Often the science fiction tale would pose ancient, almost forgotten problems on a literary stage cleared by holocaust; or it would evolve our world to a form of perfection unbearable to man, a machine-tooled sleekness dependent for sustenance on the suppression of man's life.

In this study we shall seek to enter, with our amateurs' eyes, a portion of the world of science fiction where men and women have labored for years to tell us something . . . of ourselves. Perhaps sf can lead us to a more useful approach to both present and future than we have conceived of in our various compartmentalized visions. But first we must ask: What is it?

Perhaps one's best introduction to science fiction is the pulp magazines: *Analog, IF, The Magazine of Fantasy and Science Fiction, New Worlds.* Here are occasional diamonds in the rough, fragments of fiction, the makings of novels. The sf world will begin to open. In little notes one reads of the conferences for sf devotees. One senses that there is a world of sf every bit as passionate as the worlds which congregate around the stock car tracks, the chess boards, and the bridge tables.

Doubtless, most respectable novelists hardly knew of science fiction until writers like John Barth, William Golding, and John Updike began using its conventions. Or until it burst onto the screens of the nation in *Star Trek* and *2001: A Space Odyssey.* Despite this recent interest and publicity, the pulps remain a valuable introduction because they retain the flavor of sf as it was in the 1940's and 50's—an unrespected third cousin to literature—even as they manifest both new confidence and new uncertainty in the face of the increased interest in the future and the fearsome prospect of self-annihilation through the misuse of science.

Origins

Modern science fiction can be traced to the guiding spirit of John W. Campbell, who, as editor of *Astounding* in 1937 and later as founder-editor of *Unknown* in 1939, ushered in what is sometimes referred to as the classic period of science fiction. New talent emerged and developed—Olaf Stapledon, Isaac Asimov, Robert Heinlein, Theodore Sturgeon, A. E. van Vogt, Jack Williamson, Frederik Pohl. These writers and others presented the most recent speculations of science with rich imagination at a time when the phrase "atomic age" was new. They began to construct from a diverse literary-intellectual past the fabric of space fiction and sociological prediction. Often their pessimism about the immediate future was modified by their creation of a body of literature in which the limits of technology, space, and time were greatly expanded. Men traveled to the moon and Mars, but now they also found their way to other galaxies and even to other space-time complexes. Sf heroes had traveled to worlds set 200 or 1,000 years in the future, but now they went thousands and sometimes billions of years hence to periods of time when man no longer existed and even the universe was dead or transformed into something very different.

In the late 1930's and through the 1940's, literary development of the story and of philosophical implications for the future of men were secondary in sf writing. This is not to say that these elements were not present and even outstanding in certain cases, but within the body of literature as a whole, they were secondary to the excitement of the scientifically knowledgeable imagination.

Then in the early 1950's, concern with society and the eternal questions about man, nature, and history combined with this rich imagination to produce what were exciting books on any level. A few of these are:

A Canticle for Leibowitz, Walter Miller
A Case of Conscience, James Blish
Childhood's End, Arthur C. Clarke
The Foundation (a trilogy), Isaac Asimov
More Than Human, Theodore Sturgeon
The Space Merchants, Frederik Pohl
Space Lords, Cordwainer Smith

And today a whole generation of younger science fiction writers—the "New Wave"—has burst upon the scene. With such authors as Samuel Delany, Norman Spinrad, Roger Zelazny, and James Ballard, there has come a basic change in the structure and content of the material. The treatment of character and situation has taken on increasing significance. The whole realm of scientific inquiry from parapsychology to astrophysics is being used; and the ancient devices of magic, folktale, myth, and allegory are offering new potential.

Before this period of modern science fiction, there were others who offered impressions of the interaction of men and science. There was H. G. Wells, who has the distinction of having forecast most of the major developments and problems in today's world. To his name should be added that of Jules Verne, the Frenchman whose enthusiasm for the coming era of flight and undersea exploration created works like *20,000 Leagues Under the Sea*. Although Verne was less interested in the social aspects of the future, his realization of the dangers involved in a power technology given to a not-quite-perfect man is apparent. But Wells and Verne were neither first nor alone in commenting on the impact of science upon our lives. The notion that modern men were original in their concern for the interaction of man and scientific knowledge may be corrected by a couple of examples.

Shakespeare lived in a world where already two conflicting world views were meeting in a headlong collision. The scientific optimism of the Renaissance was threatening to destroy the solid axioms of the hierarchical universe of medieval Europe. In *Romeo and Juliet* (II.iii), the apothecary-priest Friar Laurence, who mixed the sleeping potion which put Juliet to sleep, muses on the ambiguities inherent in his knowledge of herbs and plants:

> For nought so vile that on earth doth live
> But to the earth some special good doth give,
> Nor aught so good but strain'd from that fair use
> Revolts from true birth, stumbling on abuse:
> Virtue itself turns vice, being misapplied,
> And vice sometime's by action dignified.

Benjamin Franklin once wrote:

> We may perhaps learn to deprive large masses of their
> gravity, and give them absolute levity, for the sake of
> easy transport. Agriculture may diminish its labor and
> double its produce; all diseases may be . . . cured . . .
> and our lives lengthened at pleasure . . . O that men
> would cease to be wolves to one another . . .

To Franklin's positive view of science and skepticism about men, we may add the suggestion of Herman Melville's superb nineteenth-century story "The Bell Tower": that science, as the creature of man's Promethean pride, might, by behaving *as man intends it to*, destroy him almost casually in the process. Other forerunners of science fiction tended toward naïve optimism. William Harben's 1892 story "In the Year 10,000" sees technology as a simple device by which man is elevated gradually to a state of bliss.

Our century suggests that there is hardly such a correlation between man's moral betterment and "rewards" in the form of scientific progress. Indeed, it may be, as Buckminster Fuller has pointed out, that war stands behind the burgeoning scientific-technological advance of this century. The World Wars and their successors have called for advanced weaponry and support systems. War may be hell but it calls forth effort and more money with fewer questions asked than most forms of endeavor. The applied science and technology needed under pressure of war have become, by and large, the legacy of the Twentieth Century. The advances which Franklin saw coming were purchased, then, by man's failure to solve his most abiding problems. Science fiction takes this fact seriously. It has developed to maturity in the context of abiding questions posed years ago by men like Shakespeare, Franklin, and Melville.

The Themes of Science Fiction

There are numerous definitions of science fiction. It is sometimes seen as literature which has come inevitably into being as the fate of the world is seen to hang on the interaction of man and science. It is said to differ from fantasy because its scientific explanations make it *seem* plausible. Or it differs from straight fiction because it presupposes something—operative space travel, advanced cybernetics, a galactic political situation, or an environment not drawn from anyone's life experiences—that is not yet, or may never be, visibly operative in our everyday life. Perhaps science fiction is best defined, however, by an enumeration of its themes. These can be grouped into the following categories: *technological gimmickry, space travel, time travel, future scenarios,* and finally, *the exploration of inner space and ultimate meaning.*

It is possible to see a kind of progression here. Once the boundaries of scientific discovery and technology were opened up, the possibilities of space and time travel became sources for speculation. With the idea of time travel came a host of future scenarios. If there are no limits to where science and technology can take us, the possibility of realities more basic than our space-time universe can be explored. The casting aside of all the limits on what constitutes the "real" world, all those comfortable truths on which we base our conscious existence, is a giddy sensation indeed.

The first theme of science fiction, scientific and technological gimmickry, hardly need be emphasized today. But it is interesting to note that the early writers, notably Verne and Wells, accurately predicted such things as television, space travel, atomic submarines, labor-saving devices, advanced computers, and superweapons.

It is also noteworthy that such sf luminaries as Arthur C. Clarke, Isaac Asimov, and Willy Ley can claim some influence on the actual development of manned space flight. Science fiction has already anticipated many implications of man's move outward from earth. What will occur, for example, if a man is isolated on the moon or on another planet? What will be the outcome of our encounter with other life forms? If God created the universe, what would be the implication of the existence on another planet of a race of creatures who are morally perfect by the definition of the church, beings superior to men? Such a planet is envisioned in James Blish's *A Case of Conscience,* with fascinating implications for theology and existence.

Space travel opens up the new frontier, the possibility of colonizing other worlds. In science fiction, space travel is sometimes an escape from an earth grown old and war-weary, a literal new lease on life. Then there are those who take the opposite view: Space travel will be but a momentary passion of man. It will cost too much; its returns will be small. The stage of the drama will remain on earth. In *The Sirens of Titan,* Kurt Vonnegut uses countless devices to laugh, jolt, and push man to the realization that the miracles of science and space travel—miracles capable of rejuvenating man's jaded faith in the supernatural—are diversions from the essential human task: to love whoever happens to be *close* at hand. But space exploration will not be dispatched that easily, even if it serves as a modern equivalent of the Roman gladiatorial games—a diversion of the crowd from the injustices and challenges of life, life on earth, the life within. Perhaps, though, space challenges will divert the minds of nations from the business of war. The boring TV commentators who now narrate splashdowns might spice up their expositions of reality with excerpts from the searching reflections that sf has given us on the challenge of space travel.

The third theme—time travel—finds a superb example in H. G. Wells's *The Time Machine*, although there is hardly a major writer of science fiction who has not tried his hand at chronological manipulation. Quite apart from the physics and paradoxes involved in moving matter backward and forward through space and time, this device provides a means of objectifying our internal perceptions, enabling us to see the present from numerous time vantage points. The time travel story also provides a convenient means of extending plot possibilities, as the devices of magic and the supernatural did in prescientific literature.

If man can penetrate space and travel in time, what of his future? The old walls are down. An escapable globe turns in a galaxy in a universe whose outer limits are lost in conjecture. What is produced is an open future, requiring a mental readjustment in man no less wrenching than that caused by the discovery of earth's roundness or the earlier discovery—graphically portrayed in the first section of the film *2001: A Space Odyssey*—that a tool gives the vegetarian ape-man the power to kill.

It is in thought about man and his future that we find the

fourth major science fiction theme. As with space travel, so with the study of the future, sf has pioneered. The speculation that is beginning to flow from think tanks, universities, and such places as the Institute on the Future in Middletown, Connecticut, has a certain air of cold expertise. Science fiction is looser and more intuitive about the future. The scenarios one is likely to find in sf include:

a) The computer-ruled world—where all society and government is related to the existence and dominance of computers and/or robots. This world can assume many faces. It may be benign, where automated control imposes a kind of order and peace under which human freedom and dignity can develop to its full potential; where man, freed from the political and economic mechanics of life, can concentrate on those things close to him which really matter. (Enter Marshall McLuhan.) The computers permit the possibility of radical decentralization, leading to a complementary relationship between city and country and the development of a lifestyle which is oriented fundamentally toward cultural enrichment.

On the other hand, the computerized world can be tyrannical, imposing its order with a cold, inhuman glove of steel, which strips man of all decision-making power and dignity as he becomes a mere extension of the machine that rules the world.

Or, there can be a flawed order, as capricious in its operation as man himself, where man is engaged in a constant struggle to keep it "human."

A variation on the computer theme can be seen in such books as Robert Heinlein's *The Moon Is a Harsh Mistress*, where the computer actually becomes somehow "human," by developing attributes such as self-awareness and a sense of humor. This concept opens up the possibilities of man-machine symbiosis—perhaps with a human mind and consciousness wired to a computer. Could this be the next step in human evolution?

b) The world as colonizer of space—where new conditions affect man's ancient tendency toward imperialism, exploitation, and domination. The question often raised in space-colonization stories is whether or not the human race will simply repeat all the old mistakes on a much grander scale, or is it capable of a new beginning? For those who watched TV's *Star Trek* in its early days, this is a familiar theme.

c) The time of chaos—which assumes the incapacity of the present world to endure without a holocaust or some similar disaster that would clear the stage of human activity as we know it. The resulting problems could be less than pleasant, even assuming some life would remain: an atmospherically poisoned globe, the existence of mutant-monster successors to present humanity, or difficulty in reestablishing continuity with past history. Some see the chaos as ultimately beneficial, a chance to learn from experience, to start again, the resulting mutations and environmental changes giving a desirable boost to human evolution.

d) The evolutionary leap—where, through natural processes, man's evolution makes a jump in a usually desirable direction. But where does that leave *Homo sapiens*?

e) The ESP-psychic civilization—in which, either by development of innate extrasensory capacity or mutation, the widespread use of telepathy makes communication a reliable means of averting the crises that man, in the past, has created.

f) Sweeps of history—which can embrace many themes

and scenarios. This particular form provides a wide backdrop for philosophical reflection about the implications of technology and religion and about the nature of history.

There are as many future scenarios as there are sf books set in the future. Any novelist who would place his work 50 or 5,000 years beyond his own time must, of necessity, create a new environment for action. There may be the omnipresent snooping TV screens of George Orwell, the pristine test-tube breeding facilities of Aldous Huxley, or the underground and flying cities of James Blish, but, as Cordwainer Smith once observed, when one considers the effort that must be expended in creating a *plausible environment* for his readers, is it any wonder that the sf author has trouble creating *characters?* Apart from the sheer fascination of playing with future possibilities, the obvious benefit of such sf musing is to summon forth the possible conjunctions between man's action and the various worlds that may come into being.

The New Wave

By now, quite obviously, the attempt to categorize sf begins to break down. We encounter a number of writers who focus on the problem of meaning, which we referred to earlier as the exploration of *inner* space. This seems to be the trend of much contemporary science fiction. Here we find the use of old myths and legends or the apparent creation of new myths by the combining of fantasy and science fiction either in a far future setting or some timeless milieu. Such writers as Samuel Delany, Roger Zelazny, Charles Harness, Kit Reed, and Kate Wilhelm have made various attempts in this direction with varying success. The problem here is that merely because one uses names from mythology or casts a story in a vague setting does not mean that one has created a valid myth. A myth is something which grows out of a combination of old myth, history, and poetry, and endures a certain test of time because it gives some special insight into the problems of life and death. Also, it must have a story which is coherent and carries the meaning, symbolism being secondary. Ultimately it is to this trend in sf that we shall turn in our own quest for meaning.

Another aspect of the contemporary trend does not dwell on mythological names or settings, but uses the science fiction format to explore inner realities, the meaning of what is happening to us now. It differs from much of the science fiction that went before in that its purpose is less to explore the implications of the interaction between man and his science in the future world than to reflect on the things that are, or should be, going on inside of man now. At times, the scientific explanation, the traditional instrument of plausibility, is jettisoned altogether, presumably because science has proved to be on the side of materialism and other abuses of man found in today's world. As such, this literature becomes more fantasy than sf.

The somewhat schizophrenic or negative attitude which many contemporary sf writers have toward science can be seen in the title of the magazine *Fantasy and Science Fiction*, sometimes called the intellectual's sf magazine. Judith Merril, *F & SF*'s former book editor, is an ardent defender of the quest for meaning in sf, which she calls the "New Thing." She describes it as follows: "The Thing isn't so new: it is nothing more than the application of contemporary and sometimes (though mostly not very) experimental literary techniques to the kind of contemporary/experimental speculation which is the essence of science fiction." But literary technique is not the crucial ingredient. It is the taking of modern manifestations of newness into account that is important, in Judith Merril's words: "the Mothers of Invention (or the Fugs, or even the Beatles) as well as op art, student protest, psychedelics and a multiplex of other manifestations of the silly sounding phrase—Flower Power."[2]

Nihilism or a New World?

Earlier sf reflected a crisis in how man viewed his environment—what kind of a world the future held for us. Now we have, added to that, perhaps caused by it, a spiritual crisis, a crisis of meaning. In *Black Easter* by James Blish (1969) we have even an explicit death-of-God sf novel. A question which comes to mind is whether a science fiction whose subject is increasingly the problem of meaning can remain a separate compartment within literature. Perhaps it cannot. Possibly it should not. Its themes are being appropriated by the persons who would have written straight novels a generation ago. And much of the new science fiction takes on the pessimism and negativity that characterizes the vision of Western man in these decades. As such it is losing the character of popular folktale, without (in most cases) assuming the stature of myth.

The debate between the new and the old within sf rages in the columns and letters of the pulp magazines. In the November 1968 *IF* letters column, Isaac Asimov wrote:

> There is a growing tendency to delete the science from science fiction. The tendency has not borne fruit yet but it is there and I want to fight it. There are science fiction writers who think that science is a Bad Thing and that science fiction is a wonderful field in which to make this plain. This is part of a much more general attitude that Society is a Bad Thing and

must be destroyed before a new and better system can be evolved. This may strike youngsters today as a daring and novel notion, but when great-grandfather was a boy they called it Nihilism. I'm afraid I'm too square to be a Nihilist.

This, of course, is precisely the issue one must raise. Now we find ourselves confronted with a new, modern sf that shares with the young a general skepticism about the possibility of constructive meaning being found in anything from the past, including past science. Whether it is nihilism or not and whether it depends, as Asimov's letter suggests, on a dislike of science per se is another question. The real question comes back to man himself. If man is flawed, can science save him? If man's science contains destruction for us, can the evil demons be exorcized? Must skepticism about man and science lead to nihilism? Or can apparent nihilism be, in actuality, the seed of a new spirit within society capable of discerning a new world worth working and organizing for? Is the polarity that Asimov proposes too simple?

These recent trends in contemporary science fiction do not submit to easy generalization. What they do is raise questions which are—either explicitly or by implication—theological and philosophical. Are there realities—or is there a reality—more fundamental than space, time, energy, matter, or all the other words we use to designate the truths about ourselves? The seemingly avant-garde hypotheses of pessimism, so intent on throwing over past knowledge, may, on further research, move into the future to become a new world view with ancient roots. Perhaps it is the nature of our era that consciousness itself is in a process of alteration. To what extent are words like "man," "nature," and "history" terms which have atrophied and helped to distort our vision of reality? In *Babel 17*, Samuel Delany carries out an interesting investigation into the essential role of language in determining reality. In our time a covey of isolated and specialized disciplines seeks to answer essentially eclectic and wide-ranging queries relating to the very foundations of society and culture. It would seem that the typical sf writer's knowledge of science, combined with his insight into art and human nature, would place him in a highly advantageous position, at least when one considers the need to frame adequate questions.

It is a merit of science fiction that it seeks to consider all possibilities within the potentially integrating reality of the *story*. The most effective science fiction is not preachy and didactic—it is a *story*, in which our own involved reaction rather than the sermon of a character provides the meaning. If the meaningful integration of our varied experiences is hard to come by these days, it is a measure of the loss of folktale and myth in our culture. It will become clear in this study that one function of the best sf is to restore to us the possibility of regaining a mythological penetration of our one-dimensional existence. If something can be *told*, it may participate in reality. If it is true that we literally *live* by stories, by myths in the almost lost sense of the term—tales that convey a reality that no other communicative device could contain—if we live in this way, then the twin issues—nihilism versus hope, fantasy versus science—may be determined in . . . the telling of tales. By the refurbishing of our imaginations.

Two superb modern examples of science fiction embody all four elements under discussion: J. G. Ballard's *Crystal World* and Samuel Delany's *The Einstein Intersection*. Ballard's book combines almost nihilistic despair with a considerable attempt at fidelity to science. Delany's book is more hopeful, more in tune with Asimov, but does not tie hope to science. Might it not be that a healthy *agnosticism* toward science—linked as it is with today's system of doing business —is a hopeful omen for the future? The *liberation* of science might be a better goal than its obliteration. It is probably skepticism about the possibilities of such liberation under present circumstances that produces the sort of science fiction that Asimov wants to fight.

At any rate, here is science fiction, revealed as a fertile field of ideas, debate, and potential insight into ourselves, our world, our future. Our time pushes us not merely to whatever action we can take to alleviate its most glaring wrongs, but also to the task of studying new ways of putting our perceptions of reality together, ways which can lead to the revitalization of life itself.

the tortured journey
of H. G. WELLS

2

Today the younger generation has made a decision to essay the politics and/or life-style of liberation. Science fiction sometimes casts doubt on youthful idealism. Youth in some sf seem content enough if given room to ramble and freedom for the gratification of lust. In the delightfully written *A Clockwork Orange,* Anthony Burgess tunes us in to a near-future world of predatory teen-age gangs. The violence of today's world is made more open and brutal. The political powers have, in a sense, institutionalized it. The suggestion of the book is that the young hero can be saved only if his freedom to sin is preserved. But when the hero is "liberated," he lapses into the old destructive pattern. For the moment, though, it is enough to say, once again, that today's youth—some of them, a fistful of them—desire real and sweeping change. They speak of freedom and love. They have positive goals such as the liberation of blacks and the ending of militarism. But numbers and power they lack and, failing that, have they any recourse but to lapse into dropout anarchism or to plot some form of political and social revolution?

Surely political impotence is at the root of part of youth's alienation—taking politics in the very widest sense: the application of individual power to the formation of one's destiny and the molding of one's environment. The origins of this impotence may be found in the writings of H. G. Wells, the first science fiction master to use the literary form for polemical purposes—that is, to lure man into a bright new day with visions of sweet reason and technological sugar plums or to clobber him into a proper fear of the consequences of continued greed and hypocrisy. The science fiction novels of Wells contain such themes—*The Time Machine*, *The War of the Worlds* (later modernized in Orson Welles's famous fearsome broadcast), and *The First Men in the Moon*. They are striking in their uncanny grasp of the future. They also help illustrate the mentality whose failure has perhaps led to the present revolt of white Western youth against the values and system of their parents.

In 1931, Wells, progressively more discouraged by society's failure to implement the humanistic reforms he so delighted in proposing, wrote: "Gladly would the prophet prophesy pleasant things." He was predicting the shape of the world in 1981, and the view was unpleasant: "He sees a world still firmly controlled by soldiers, patriots, usurers, and financial adventurers; a world surrendered to suspicion and hatred, losing what is left of its private liberties very rapidly, blundering towards bitter class conflicts and preparing for new wars . . ."[1]

What was Wells's program? He had many. In 1932 he proposed a series of voluntary societies whose main tenet would be the withdrawal of allegiance to nations. These small groups would work toward the abolition of weapons, the socialization of economics, and the development of a world organization capable of building new societies on a massive scale. The ideals were commendable: universal education, humane penology, the elimination of virulent nationalism.

The details are outlined in *After Democracy*. But the nub of Wells's problem, at least superficially, lay in numbers. He closes his grand social proposal with the furtive statement that the societies will seek their ends "irrespective of the number of . . . supporters." What he could not solve, then, was *the problem of means*, the problem plaguing every liberal Westerner who has sought to reform twentieth-century society: how to gain authority, power.

A portion of the contemporary New Left solves the problem by pushing for a pattern of decentralization in which autonomous local groups become the most important units of action, and by a style that de-emphasizes traditional organization and hierarchical leadership. But to date the New Left has failed to produce reform. Indeed, we should have no New Left were it not for the failure of conventional democratic politics to produce substantive change. So we have the spectacle of U Thant predicting doom and U.S. citizens living in sufficient satisfaction to make changes in areas of economic, racial, and military policies somewhat unlikely.

The numbers answer is too simple. Why are the numbers dedicated to constructive change so small? To be sure, there are conflicts concerning the sort of society that is desired. Some would preserve competition even if there were no rational reason for it in an abundant economy. Others would prefer totally new forms of family organization and communal life. Optimum choice for all seems the goal of all goals. But other questions intervene: With the best goal in the world, how do you get there? Not by orderly politics, evidently. Man may not be built to change that way. "And to harangue him so grandiosely as does Wells in the hope of bringing about vast changes and improvements in his actions and state, is to address one who stands at best startled and confused by life . . . He does not know . . . the direction in which life is moving. Nor can he be shown." That at least is the opinion of Theodore Dreiser in his introduction to Wells's novel *Tono-Bungay*.

To compound the reformer's difficulty, there is the reality of violence. If persuasion fails and urgency persists, is there some moral right that devolves upon the person who knows "what is best" for all mankind? Can he, in good conscience, overpower and manipulate his opponents, taking heart from Machiavelli's sage dictum "All unarmed Prophets have been destroyed"? What of the willingness of the revolutionary to encourage existing tendencies toward violence in order to mold the resulting chaos into a more tolerable order? All such violence might be justified on a "greatest good for the greatest number" ethic . . . if there were someone around who could prove that the violence actually reaped more "good" than evil. Wells, at any rate, did not live to take part in these latter-day arguments. Isaac Asimov records:

> As the years passed, Wells grew older, sicker, and more pessimistic. The manner in which the western nations allowed themselves to sink, shortsightedly, into the abyss of World War II, and the mass destruction of that war (which Wells had described with uncanny accuracy in several of his science fiction stories) completed his disillusionment.[2]

Is it any wonder that messages of joy are hard to sing out in the White West? Is it not possible to understand the tendency of churches, homes, schools, to cling to the "good things" in the culture out of fear, the fear that would come from a naked analysis of modern man's predicament? The good he would do, he seemingly cannot; the evil he would avoid seems to lie at his doorstep.

Wells illuminates the predicament of man's impotence but does not solve it. George Orwell saw its resolution in *1984* in a power stalemate with pointless war serving as a basic outlet for energy, the central *raison d'être* and the economic base. Aldous Huxley portrayed *Brave New World* as the locus of a cynically applied pharmacy designed to regulate every phase of a life of inherent boredom. If today's youth had no injustice to stoke their revolutionary defiance, they could easily turn science fiction warnings into a convincing argument for the creation of immediate chaos or the flight from "reality" via drugs and a return to nature. One wonders too whether the official gratification of individual desires (let us say, the legalization and widespread use of pot) might have the hidden side effect of making it easier for some future government to impose an Orwellian version of "law and order." Ah, the difficult game that Jacob Brackman's generation will play: a chess game with pieces labeled slavery and freedom, these labels to be revealed only at checkmate.

The dominant tendency of the social science fiction which followed Wells is to remind us at once of realistic barriers to human progress and to suggest that man possesses more endurance than we are likely to give him credit for. An example of this is the work of Frederik Pohl. Pohl can be viewed in one sense as a direct descendant of Wells in terms of his warnings about the society in which we live. He is, however, a more ebullient, satirical personality, who evinces a bit more hope, despite his frustration with social and economic structures and his skepticism over the possibility of change. In his book of short stories *The Man Who Ate the World*, he deals with the ultimate implications of the society of abundance, suggesting the insanity of a system whose welfare depends on ever increasing consumption. *The Space Merchants*, written by Pohl and C. M. Kornbluth, pursues this theme further. A society plagued with problems of over-population and overurbanization is completely controlled by the advertising industry. The ethics and false loyalties of Madison Avenue dominate human relationships. Although set in the future, this story deals directly with the problem of today—the forces which inhibit personal freedom in subtle and not-so-subtle ways. The resolution of *Space Merchants* occurs when a man faces up to the "system," fighting it on its own terms and thus "saving" himself and a remnant of others who see the dehumanizing effect and ultimate self-destruction of such a society.

Much modern social science fiction makes plausible a stage through which humanity passes, a stage which prostrates man (at least temporarily) to a tide of dehumanization and conformity—to the worst features of the technetronic society. Totalitarianism (in the sense of removing from man the freedom to "sin") is the essence of most of these new orders. The root assumption is that survival on the planet is dependent upon the imposition of some sort of control based on technique, technology, science. It is instructive that such an assumption is plausible to us. We seem ready to accept a future in which the chaos brought about by rapid social change is harnessed by such means. We see, possibly, that totalitarian scenes in science fiction are actually objectifications of a general psychic state of anticipation in today's world.

Heroism, in science fiction, can involve the necessity of an ultimate faceoff with systems that stifle man, as in *The Space Merchants* or Robert Heinlein's *Revolt in 2100*, but the hero can also be the one who imposes a "perfect order" on man "for his own good." In the latter case, the power to overcome sin, previously reserved to God, is assumed by men who have gained omniscience and omnipotence by means of applied science. One detects here the basis of ambivalence toward science and technology. On one hand, the future is the stage upon which man plays God, rationalizing the world, only to be forced—eventually—to fight his new creation in order to regain his lost soul. On the other hand, science and technology make possible the overcoming of precisely the kinks that have made "the system" unworkable in the past. Science aids man to victory. In the first case, the enemy is seen as the tendency toward the reduction of "all varieties of temperament and desire to one universal system of thought and behavior" (Herbert Read). Whether this is accomplished by computer domination or by the handiwork of an elite is unimportant. The crucial assumption is that the stable utopia is a chimera, a structure that must topple. In the second case, the situation is precisely reversed. The traitor becomes the person who would thwart the progress of man's science and technology toward omnipotence and omniscience. The hero is a sort of decontaminated, robust, and relatively uncomplicated Nietzschean superman.

So, who finally is the traitor and who the hero? We are left with a paradox.

The paradox of rationalism and freedom moves us beyond Wells's problem of means, for now the most desirable ends are thrown into doubt. Order or freedom? Or is man capable of having both? Ultimately the question moves to the nature of man and history. No resolution can take place until the human drama has been advanced beyond its present stage in history. Precisely for this reason the future-orientation of sf is useful.

In biblical terms, reform is always the first word of the prophet; the prognostication of disaster is the second: "O Jerusalem, Jerusalem, killing the prophets and stoning those who are sent to you! How often would I have gathered your children together as a hen gathers her brood under her wings, and you would not!" (Matthew 23:37). The paradox can be expressed in several ways: the conflict between those who maintain that the Kingdom of God is exclusively on earth, and those who see its realization in another resurrected world; the City of Man versus the City of God; the notion of the church as the new community or the herald of that community set against the view that the institutional church is quite irrelevant to the outcome of the human drama. Theologically, as in sf, the paradox is never quite resolved.

If reform of the Wells variety (response to the prophet's first word) seems an unlikely prospect and if violence is counterproductive, one is forced to hope (in secular terms) for two developments: revolution in which old power realities are altered to permit humane reordering (but the altering of old power realities may involve violence), or cultural revolution in which a basic change in human consciousness becomes the motive power for positive reform. Political and cultural revolutionaries are beginning to sort themselves out as the younger generation moves toward its various Armageddons. Perhaps a new cultural-political synthesis will emerge to save the political approach from nihilism and the cultural vision from naïveté. We know for certain only that some change will be necessary to convert today's precarious idealism into tomorrow's reality. The sad story of H. G. Wells suggests that a difficult passage awaits us as we strive to enter the new world that is upon us. Like a good companion or counselor on a space era pilgrim's progress, science fiction leaves us to find our way. But it helps us to phrase the questions we will need, eventually, to answer.

Now we shall turn from survey to analysis, seeing what

particular works of sf have to say on the questions of man, nature, and history. Hopefully, such an approach will stimulate debate among long-term sf buffs and interest among those whose acquaintance with this literature is casual.

HUMANUM:
what manner of men are we?

3

> When I search for Man in the technique and the style of Europe, I see only a succession of negations of man, and an avalanche of murders. . . . Humanity is waiting for something other from us than such an imitation . . . For Europe, for ourselves and for humanity, comrades, we must turn over a new leaf, we must work out new concepts, and try to set afoot a new man.
>
> —FRANTZ FANON[1]

The call of the prematurely deceased African psychiatrist Frantz Fanon is the cry of two-thirds of the world against the West, insofar as the West represents oppressive imperialism and colonialism rather than democracy and humanity. It is the call of a man acutely and existentially aware of the *reason* for the failure of reformers like Wells to convince the West to change its ways. There were, indeed, roots of the "negation of man" in the oppressive political systems of imperialism and fascism, but they could not be pulled out merely by calling them bad. There were causes for the failure of reformers to group their strength effectively, but the reformers could hardly bear the full guilt for the failure of the West to alter itself constructively. No, the answer was elsewhere.

In the Bible, violence had been a usual feature of triumphant liberation and attainment of new life. But liberation had depended not upon violence per se, but rather on the fulfillment of what Fanon sees as the basic need: the creation of a new man whose identity was no longer dependent on subservience to the old masters. How great the difference between the cliché that social morality stems from individual conversion and Fanon's tortured cry of practically the same thing: that revolution for the sake of human betterment cannot take place without a 180-degree turn within mankind itself!

As if to acknowledge the need for *some* newness in man, the World Council of Churches called in 1968 for a major evaluation throughout the churches of "the humanum"—of man. The Council said: "Scientific discoveries and the revolutionary movements of our time open new potentialities and perils for men. Man is lost because he does not know who he is."

If Fanon provides the revolutionaries' reason for man's inability to know himself, to face himself, science fiction serves to explain the predicament even further. Economic injustice is not the theme of most science fiction. But, interestingly, we shall see emerging from a study of how some sf writers look at man a set of implications no less "revolutionary" than those with which Fanon closes his book *The Wretched of the Earth*.

In passing now from casual reference to sf books to the precarious attempt to suggest the content of specific works, we must risk distorting the authors' meanings, and for that we take full responsibility. We are, in effect, *using* science fiction as a means of refining our own, and, hopefully, the reader's, thinking.

Born of Man . . . but Different

A veteran sf author who can tell us something of man is A. E. van Vogt, who has produced creditable work for more than three decades. *Slan*, his story of mutants on earth, first appeared as a serial in 1940. The slans are creatures born of man, but endowed with features and intelligence marking them as *different*. Van Vogt has the creatures persecuted by mankind for more than a millennium before they devise a means of disguising themselves, at which point they are able to carry forth a nonviolent genetic revolution.

Van Vogt's slans are essentially products of evolution. "What happened seemed simply to have been a reaction to the countless intolerable pressures that were driving men mad, because neither their minds nor their bodies were capable of withstanding modern civilization."[2] Slans must arrive if "humanity" is to survive. Although born of man, they are persecuted because of their difference. In a later book, *The Universe Maker*, van Vogt explains the evolution of certain future social structures with the following remark:

> The pressure of civilization was apparently too much for millions of people. It turned out to be a combination of inherited weakness and justified withdrawal from intolerable pressure. But man can build any civilization he desires. So the problem is to free him by mollifying the experiences and disasters that had befallen the affected protoplasmic lines.[3]

The twentieth century is seen as the beginning point in a psychological disaster for man which leaves him demoralized and unable to cope with life.

We see here not the fallen man of conservative Christianity who can be redeemed by a simple confession of faith and whose ultimate destiny is resurrection beyond this tragic earth. Nor is van Vogt suggesting that man is done in by some outside agency or natural disaster. No, man must change or perish because the environment he has created has become too much for him. He is the author of his own dilemma. And yet, his problem will not be solved by an increase in intelligence, although the slans—van Vogt's next step after man—are highly intelligent. No, what must take place is massive evolution in the power to communicate and to comprehend what is going on inside of another person, and it is this power that bodes well for the future. The mutant slans can read minds, a fact which increases insight into psychology and capacity for education and adaptation. History can continue.

Another mutation story is Theodore Sturgeon's *More Than Human*. It takes the need for closer communication even further. Five children, all outcasts of one sort or another, but all with some unusual attribute, band together in a symbiotic relationship which gives them a total being superior to the sum of their parts. The evolutionary process is at work; *Homo sapiens* is to be replaced by *Homo gestalt*. However, *Homo gestalt* is not complete and cannot survive until it has acquired an ethos. Sturgeon describes this ethos:

> What it is really is a reverence for your sources and your posterity. It is a study of the main current which created you, and in which you will create still a greater thing when the time comes . . . Help humanity . . . and humanity will help you, for it will produce more like you, and then you will no longer be alone . . . And when there are enough of your kind, your ethics will be their morals.[4]

The thing which completes Sturgeon's new creature is the ethical sense, and with it comes a feeling of shame, something presumably the single human lacked. After shame comes self-respect and joy in being a part of humanity. The final implication of the story is that the ultimate goal of the human evolutionary process is one grand *Homo gestalt*, encompassing all humanity. Then there would be no more point in struggling and hurting one another. Although probably not intended as such, this story can be seen as an sf rendering of the concept of brotherhood. That which injures one, injures all; that which aids one, aids all, whether dealing with a family or nations.

The notion, from the human perspective, that we might look to our perpetuation in mutants among us is scandalous; it offends us because it seems to undermine the minimal concept of our own individual worth that ought to be the basis of whatever victory we might win in life. In the van Vogt novel, slans are persecuted. Men invent wild hypotheses to escape the reality of the slans' human origin. In Sturgeon's *More Than Human*, the new form is viewed with suspicion and repulsion, as something "unnatural" and dangerous.

The psychological trauma of dealing with the "new man" is not new in history. Perhaps the most elaborate analysis of this phenomenon is found in Christian theology. For some, the notion of Christ born of a mere human being is scandalous. But for others the notion that the child of Mary is the first fruit of a new, God-inspired humanity is the affront. One begins to understand that Christ's newness, his very difference, his strange new power, is the impetus for the subsequent theological argument. How to explain the new man? The notion that salvation lies in taking on the form of, or incorporating, the new man is sensible enough if one perceives that man in his natural state is incapable of attaining personal or social salvation. In our time the notion of the new man has often led not to passivity and world-denial, but to precisely the opposite: the assumption that the new man is the one who takes history into his own hands and builds it up for the sake of himself and his brothers. Such a posture involves a reinterpretation of the mutant, Christ-human, yet something else as well—a willingness to seek means of reconciling the attempt to "control" history with the need to grant man autonomy, including the autonomous freedom to reject the new order.

There is little question that our period is one of messianic expectations; indeed, there may soon arise varieties of messiahs consistent with the diversity of expectations. Science fiction contributes to messianic hope the notion of mutation, which can be taken either literally and biologically or symbolically, as an expression of inner longing. The desire for fundamental change shows up politically in the revolutionary spirit, and also in the preoccupation with the numerous pseudo-religions and practices that have sprung up to gratify man's quest for meaning. The search for identity has not waited for initiatives from bodies like the World Council of Churches or the United Nations, or even from the less remote traditional institutions of the church and the school. If some contemporary efforts at self-realization are pathetic, they are at the same time signs of the extent to which the formal society and established religion no longer offer man a mirror in which he can find his true self.

Another dimension raised in these mutation stories concerns the status of possible new forms of humanity. It may be that man, with his passion for classification, will have to suspend judgment or develop utterly new modes of self-definition, should mutations become common rather than exceptional. Debate on such questions would lead one inevitably to the ways in which modern man already creates distinctions within humanity—genocidal distinctions based on race, ideology, and economic level.

The distinction between man and animal has been made both philosophically and scientifically, though both scientists and philosophers recognize man's animal origins. Konrad Lorenz, in *On Aggression*, ties the man-beast knot very tightly indeed, and goes on to suggest that, in the light of this, laughter may prove our only defense against self-annihilation.[5] If, however, man is distinct from the animal, what would mankind do in the face of *others* seeming or claiming to represent an advanced form of humanity, perhaps as advanced as man is over the ape? One puts the question in exaggerated form, but is it not possible that a world of the very rich and the very poor, such as that envisioned by C. P. Snow in his forecasts of mass starvation, might force man, in order to preserve his sanity, to make distinctions within humanity on the basis of who deserves to survive? Such a distinction might even be on the basis of the cliché "Judge a man on his merits." This could result in a new version of the Calvinistic concept of equating wealth and merit.

Again we have underlined the importance as well as the extreme complexity of arriving at a just means of defining man. Needless to say, if it came to survival, Fanon would have a rather different definition of what constitutes a new and worthy humanity than, let us say, the military-industrial-university complex. Perhaps there is a revolutionary meaning in the remark of Jesus concerning judgment. "Judge not, that you be not judged"! The suggestion is that God, not man, defines the human.

Robert Heinlein and the Strong Stranger

Any examination of science fiction would be incomplete without a visit with that lusty veteran Robert A. Heinlein. His book *Stranger in a Strange Land* has become something of a bible to some within that diverse movement variously referred to as the New Left or the hippies. *Stranger* is the story of a man born and orphaned on Mars and raised by Martians, who is found and brought back to earth. His Martian upbringing has left him with extraordinary telepathic abilities; he can read thoughts, leave his body, and control matter. On earth he forms a "religion," or movement, which includes instruction in the Martian language and these same telepathic powers. Martian is much more logical than any earth language, and contains structures and thought forms which make the learning of telepathy possible. His followers gather in communes or "nests"—ten or fifteen people living together in a close-knit, sexually free-flowing, family relationship. Within the nest they grow in understanding of one another, at the same time carrying on their own education in Martian and telepathy. They proceed to initiate others into the mysteries—starting new "nests." Out of this sexually satisfying and consciousness-expanding relationship presumably will come the "new man," wiser and more humane, who will survive to replace all the poor restless clods milling around, aimlessly killing each other off, out in the streets. The various telepathic and teleporting abilities (including the capacity to make an undesirable object or person disappear) definitely give them a certain survival advantage over others. The man from Mars is finally crucified by an angry mob and passes into some nondescript, corporation-style heaven whose function is to run the universe and where it is made plain that all men are God.

Passing over the whimsy which pervades this book and accepting the inoffensive, often delightful joy Heinlein gets in discussing good food and good sex, some fairly interesting opinions about the nature of man come to the fore here as in his other books.

As with so many other sf writers, Heinlein is concerned about man's flawed powers of communication. Language itself is illogical and awkward, forcing man to espouse ideas which are less than what they should be. In both *Stranger* and an earlier short story, "Gulf," a new streamlined (but also richer) language must be learned before history can be changed for the better. In a later book, *The Moon Is a Harsh Mistress*, a genial computer takes over the thought-communication process and plans and organizes a complete revolution. Although the human thought-communication process is flawed, Heinlein implies that we, or at least some of us, have it in our power to do something about it. Hopefully, too, telepathic powers would emerge to facilitate the process.

Another related Heinlein theme concerns the need for more satisfying, flexible family structures. We have the example of the "nest" in *Stranger*. A more intriguing one, which takes into account growing children of various ages, is the "line marriage" found in *The Moon Is a Harsh Mistress*. Here several men and women of various ages live together as a family; as older ones die, younger ones are taken in. Children leave the family when of marriageable age to join other lines. In this way it differs from the patriarchal or matriarchal extended families as well as from the familiar atomistic family of our own suburban day.

However, in spite of these typically appealing and often worthwhile themes, there is another aspect of Heinlein, which we find disturbing. This is what we will call his elitist or "subjective meritocratic" tendency. Believing that society, by eliminating the rough and tough process of natural selection (a la Darwin) from its history, has opened the door to the survival of inferior stock, Heinlein suggests that "inferior" people may end up dragging the rest of humanity down with them by their stupidity, laziness, and moral flabbiness. This is expressed in *Stranger* as follows: ". . . here babies do not compete [as on Mars] but adults do; on Mars adults never compete, they've been weeded out as babies. But one way or another, competing and weeding takes place . . . or a race goes downhill." Religion is partially to blame for the decline of man: "No matter what I said they insisted on thinking of God as something outside themselves. Something that yearns to take every indolent moron to His breast and comfort him. The notion that the effort has to be *their own* . . . and that the trouble they are in is all their own doing . . . is one that they can't or won't entertain."[6] In *The Moon*, the difficulty of survival in a hostile environment provided, in less than 200 years, a population with strengths greater than those on earth, even though it had been originally colonized solely by criminals and other rejects of society.

The implications of this kind of thinking can be seen more obviously in the earlier mentioned story "Gulf." The head of the benevolent secret society of superior human beings states the main theme: "Joe, didn't you ever feel the yen to wipe out some evil, obscene, rotten jerk, who infected everything that he touched, yet was immune to legal action? We treat them as cancers; we excise them from the body social. We keep a 'Better Dead' list; when a man is clearly morally bankrupt we close his account at the first opportunity."[7]

What tends to emerge—social Darwinism? meritocracy?— is a society in which positive characteristics are preserved and those which are regarded as less than useful are siphoned off.

One suspects from reading Heinlein that, in spite of his belief in rugged individualism and his suspicion of the liberal's well-meaning tinkering with society which threw the natural processes out of balance, *he* might relish the opportunity to create a society (or be the man behind a charismatic leader who would) *if it could be done along his lines.*

One way to look at this view is to see how it resembles what theologians call the Deuteronomic concept of history. This view, drawn from the book of Deuteronomy in the Bible, runs as follows: There is a standard of virtue; a Force acts to reward those who abide by the standard and to condemn those who violate it. Portions of the Old Testament seek to mold history into a formal Deuteronomic framework, even though history is seldom that neat. Good men win; bad men lose. The psalmists offer the corrective: Good men suffer, the wicked prosper—why, O Lord, why? In Heinlein we find an objectification of the Deuteronomic notion—a power is erected which executes judgment in the here and now. The "better dead" list is an interesting reminder of the "omnipotence" which some men have possessed in the past and, indeed, possess in our time. Of course, what Heinlein is seeking to solve is the problem of evil within history, and the theory he advances is merely a variation on the quite respectable thought of such Cold War philosophers as Columbia University's Zbigniew Brzezinski. Society must be managed by a new class; misfits must be controlled; dissidents must be eliminated. Ironically, there are also links between Heinlein's thought and the covenant concept which formed the essential dynamic of American Puritanism, the first generation of which constituted a theocracy. Banishment was one Puritan means of quelling dissent.

Heinlein's elites must improve themselves, however, before assuming the responsibilities they desire. But ordinary man cannot learn these new things because he lacks the discipline, the *will*, to do so. Only the elite can "fiddle with issues of racial life and death" ("Gulf," p. 61).

Think about that for a moment!

Isn't this precisely what the twentieth century is all about? Having killed, forgotten, or grown beyond God, man contemplated his own responsibility for the universe, seemingly without a Judge. Is it not moral for "wise men" to fill the vacuum? Heinlein's stories suggest that there is only one answer. The author asks whether man as presently constituted can make it—whether he can move beyond the present into a future without the formidable evils of our own time. And his reason forces him to an elitist solution. There are already those among us whose intelligence and superior will make them the natural guardians of man and his future. They must be given power soon, or we face a series of totalitarian repressions (presumably aimed at the Heinlein elite as well as other nonconformists). How tempting are such notions! We are less honest than Heinlein if we deny their basic appeal. If only we (people like us!) could take over, we could run the world so much better . . .

Such may be the mentality of disappointed reformers. No doubt the world can use more intelligence and healthy willpower, but is there any evidence that there is in some men the kind of intelligence which, once it has gained power, would guarantee more humane actions than are presently taken?

Heinlein emerges as science fiction's Ayn Rand, only her industrialists are replaced by his scientists, telepaths, and scrappy computer mechanics. But again a caution. Heinlein has suggested a very real possibility, redemptive or chilling depending on your point of view or, rather, your exposure to the world as it is. In a time of increasing human capacity for the creation of chaos (official, unofficial), the question of who calls the shots is of critical importance. Or at least that is what we tend to believe. Dostoevsky once observed that if God is dead, all things are possible. Heinlein accepts the sf viewpoint that all things are possible and occupies himself with the question of human salvation in the light of this observation. The contrast which Dostoevsky creates is between the worship of man and the worship of God. Heinlein's world is divided between reasoning moral men and unreasoning immoral men.

It is interesting that Heinlein has anticipated the hippie movement in *Stranger in a Strange Land*. The irony is that "love children" can be just as judgmental in their basic perspective as any other self-styled elites. What is lacking in Heinlein and in elitist thought generally is a standard of justice which applies equally to the high and the low—to all men. Even if such a standard cannot be legislated, it is a necessary antidote to the perversions of elitist totalitarianism.

There is much to admire, much to criticize in Heinlein's proposed societies, but the basic issue remains: What constitutes the ultimate standard of judgment—or principle of criticism—in a consciously imposed (even if benevolent) meritocracy? The notion of meritocracy, which in an ideal world would simply be the provision of fulfillment to all through the realization of individual talents and desires, must be evaluated in terms of the actual disparities within wealthy nations and of growing gaps between well-to-do and poor nations.

(For more understanding of the problems of meritocracy see Michael Young's *The Rise of the Meritocracy, 1870-2033*,

Random House, 1959; and *The Academic Revolution,* by
Christopher Jencks and David Riesman, Doubleday, 1968,
pp. 12, 97, 146-147.)

Beyond Merit

There seems to be no lack of insight within man as to
what he or, most often, others *ought* to do; there is even a
tendency to so burden himself (and others) with such impossible obligations that he becomes incapable of the slightest
remedial action. Such legalism or "super-egoism" is recognized
in Christian thought as the inevitable companion of a closed
human system which takes judgment unto itself. The biblical
doctrine of justification by faith, properly perceived as forgiveness in the face of failure to meet *legitimate* demands,
is Christianity's way of suggesting a means of freeing man
from his predicament of guilt fed by the failure to do what he
knows he should do. In Heinlein, *guilt* is not the barrier to
effective performance. The need is for appropriate disciplined
action, by *those capable of it.* Sloth, rather than a condition
of impotence resulting from guilt, would be the fundamental
characteristic of the "worthless" folk in Heinlein's books.

Sloth—*acedia*—is one of the seven cardinal sins within
Catholic tradition, but a strand of contemporary secular theology tends to elevate sloth as *the* basic manifestation of sin
in today's world. This leads to a concept of worthiness as
participation in the upbuilding of a just society—precisely the
ideal of the reformer. This tendency of secular theologians to
agree with Heinlein on the basic sin is partly the result of a
need to jettison the false but popular notion of sin as private
misdeeds (usually sexual) that is endemic in the United
States. But one must ask whether a more Catholic concept
of sin, combined with a more authentically Protestant (icono-

clastic) stance against all forms of idolatry, is not a needed corrective to the commendable but somewhat naïve focus of secular theology. The late Karl Barth was often criticized because his theology emphasized that the redemption of man lay wholly beyond human initiative, and that men—all men— were sinful. But, it seems, in retrospect, that Barth was a good deal more trenchant and accurate in his social criticism than were many theologians who sought to justify theology in terms of its direct relevance to human problems. Proper theology does not suggest a code of ethics, how to behave in the face of a particular problem, but a human stance that is at once iconoclastic and constructionistic.

Hardly any sf writer entertains a wholly optimistic view of man's nature. Whether man is seen as a stage in the evolutionary process or as a weak personality, human frailty of some sort is assumed. Indeed, in many cases it is weakness, cupidity, and aggression within man that give rise to a highly apocalyptic sf perspective. If the church has distorted the meaning of Original Sin, one is tempted to suggest that the Genesis tale of Adam's trespass (and its numerous interpretations) is alive and well . . . in science fiction if not theology.

Beyond Intelligence

We have pointed out the difficulty of finding the perfect intelligence and will in any man. Imagine for the moment that such a thing is possible, and science functioned properly. Would it not be possible that unseen problems could arise? Theodore Sturgeon raised this question very early in his short story "Microcosmic God," written in 1941. A brilliant biochemist—without an ounce of megalomania or hostility toward his fellows—isolates himself on an island and creates beyond the range of the easily conceivable. The culmination of this inventiveness is a new race of tiny men whose evolution is speeded up so that the scientist can have access to knowledge that would otherwise require a wait of centuries. When the biochemist is finally threatened by a greedy associate, he has his creatures invent a shield which can protect them from human interference for as long as they want to be protected. We are left with the possible emergence, at some unforeseen point in history, of an infinitely superior man-created race which has no reason for benevolence toward its creators. This story, far from being an argument for placing control in the hands of the most advanced people, is testimony to the possibility of man-created forces that exceed the bounds of human control. Might not man be victimized, finally, by the very intelligence that should be his saving grace? Or is there a power or corrective beyond intelligence more promising in its consequences for the future? Sturgeon's tale harks back to Melville, but is almost more chilling, because of its implication that disinterested, intelligently guided science may exceed man's control. Obviously, Sturgeon, in *More Than Human*, sees the need for an ethos, a standard, a preparation, which can embrace some of the far-reaching changes progress and intelligence may bring. To bring this closer to home, shouldn't we be preparing ourselves in some way for the implications of such scientific advances as organ transplants, the extension of individual human life, and the creation of life itself?

Beyond Love?

We have discussed aspects of man's evolution and destination, the centrality of improved communication, the ambiguities inherent in his intelligence and scientific knowledge, the problems of the will, and the need for some transcendent standard to counter the impulse toward totalitarian elitism.

But—Christians, Beatles, and Flower Children may cry—what of love? Is not the essence and salvation of man his ability to love? Thus far we have avoided discussion of the one characteristic that much Christian tradition regards as the most valued sign of grace in man.

It is love that has informed the ethic of movements for human justice after other possible bases of change have collapsed. Whether the soul-force of Gandhi or the nonviolence of Martin Luther King is under discussion, the fundamental social power which we can describe as love-in-action depends upon a willingness to give life itself for the brethren. Interestingly, both Gandhi and King emerged in reaction to the failure of other sorts of reforming effort; both acted in response to the unrenewability of their societies; both came to see their "ways" as means of infusing the oppressed with a new breath of vitality. Theirs was the road beyond reform politics and armed revolution. The third alternative.

Perhaps one may distinguish between two sorts of voluntarism: the formal voluntarism of an H. G. Wells, which seeks by orderly means and the application of intelligence and persuasion to change society for the better; and the *voluntarism of love*, which is fundamentally sectarian and movement-centered and which depends less on intelligence than on intangibles like endurance, the willingness to absorb suffering, and the capacity to use shame and embarrassment as a weapon in the struggle. It seems, in 1970, that the first sort of voluntarism carries within it, perhaps unconsciously, an implied will to control the destiny of those who are being "helped"; it partakes of paternalism, an overbearing and gratuitous social posture. Perhaps it is this trait that Dreiser discerns in Wells when he says that man will not likely follow the preachments of the volatile Englishman. It is this tendency we see in Heinlein. But what Dreiser may miss and Heinlein may see is the change that takes place in man when the first form of voluntarism fails. When society is "beyond reform," man then entertains a certain pessimism about himself or the "others," and about progress in general, determining that justice will not be won without direct action of some sort. Enter Heinlein's elite. Enter nonviolent love-in-action.

The voluntarism of love seems to emerge when intolerable situations exist. The power of love is then expressed in a public manifestation of weakness and conscience-inspiring submission to the worst depredations of the oppressor. In the last few years, many have reached the conclusion that we have passed the time when either form of voluntarism is efficacious. But the voluntarism of love is capable of surviving in the world, even if the vehicle for its effectiveness is temporarily shattered—as it was during the last part of Dr. King's career. When the society renders the voluntarism of love ineffective, a split may take place between those who would seek to discern the dimensions of love in other phenomena (personal, sexual relationships, Flower Power, separation from society) and those who believe that, regardless of love's merits, there is a time for judgment in history, represented in the formation of a politically revolutionary, possibly violent ideology. Whether out of this new division there emerges a new synthesis, one can hardly say.

Two dimensions of love emerge, then: One is a sense of brotherhood, the social, historical dimension; the other is personal, the revitalizing force each person encounters, hopefully, at some points in his life. One can be a social force for reforming the environment, the other inspires the search for inner meaning.

In the writings of the late Cordwainer Smith we find rich examples of the first and keys to the second. Cordwainer Smith (who once credited Jesus as being "the greatest psychiatrist of them all" and the man who taught him to love animals) gives us a potentially saving version of love in his admirable sf adaptation of the Joan of Arc story, "The Dead Lady of Clown Town." Set far in the future, on some planet in a long-since-colonized galaxy, Smith's Joan is the leader of the "underpeople"—creatures half human, half animal, originally bred to do the manual labor for which robots were unequipped. The "underpeople" are now the victims of a society that runs along rather smoothly and boringly. The underpeople wage a war of love against their oppressors. "You are my brother, even though my blood is rat blood," cries one combatant as she falls from the blow of her assailant. *"I love you, soldier.* We share a common speech, common hopes, common fears, and a common death. That is what Joan has taught us all. Death is not bad, soldier. . . . you will remember me after you have killed me and my babies. You will remember that I love you now—"[8]

Joan brings the people what she calls *life-with:* "It's more than love. Love's a hard, sad, dirty word, a cold word, an old word. It says too much and it promises too little." And again: "If you're alive, you're alive. If you're alive-with, then you know the other life is there too—both of you, any of you, all of you. Don't do anything. Don't grab, don't clench, don't possess. Just *be.* That's the weapon. There's not a flame or a gun or a poison that can stop it" (p. 75).

It is a love called life-with that defines true humanity for Smith—that and an indifference to death. Perhaps a similar life-with and death indifference emerges from the heart of a properly apprehended Christianity. It remains to wrest that possibility from the ashes of the acculturated church, but it may be precisely the power that can lead the needed liberation and put meaning into life.

C. S. Lewis's "Bent" World

The late C. S. Lewis—English theologian, wit, man of letters—is the only science fiction writer whose intentions appear overwhelmingly theological and didactic. While many sf stories deal with theology, none seem to have the evident purpose of Lewis's: the presentation of a formal "apology" for a certain body of Christian doctrine.

Lewis's space trilogy—*Out of the Silent Planet, Perelandra,* and *That Hideous Strength*—is a case in point. Three men representing respectively the "saved" Christian, the wicked-possessed, and the worldly egotist journey to Mars and find three forms of intelligent life living in harmony: *sorns* (the scientists and intellectuals); *hrossa* (poets, musicians, fishermen); *pfifltriggi* (craftsmen, miners, sculptors). The divisions are meant to suggest a conception of unfallen man: rational mind; refined emotion; physical activity, constructively channeled. The three groups are under the leadership of the good spirit, Oyarsa. With a race of immortal souls, spirit forms called *eldila,* he sees that the affairs of the three groups proceed in a problem-free manner. All runs smoothly; there is no need for politics; there is no conflict between these widely different forms.

In contrast, men are presented as "bent," distorted, suspicious, greedy, and aggressive—evil. Why is man this way? The *eldil* who is in charge of the earth is "bent"—he corresponds to one Christian conception of the devil. He is the embodiment of what the New Testament calls the "principalities and powers" which stand between man and his attainment of true freedom, salvation, life itself. According to the good spirit Oyarsa, there are laws which all intelligent beings know—"pity and straight dealing and shame and the like, and one of these is the love of kindred." Earth's bent spirit ruler has "taught you to break all of them except this one . . . this one he has bent until it becomes folly . . ."[9] The Martians—clearly meant to embody an old but unfallen world—have no fear of death. But not in the fiercely life-affirming manner of Cordwainer Smith's characters. On Mars, the death-fearlessness stems from resigned submission to the "true God" Maledil and to the nature of things; thus their lives are peaceful, unworried, and productive.

On one level this story presents the science fiction theme of the encounter of alien species, an exciting possible by-product of space travel. If we chose to draw allegory or meaning from the other sf books we have discussed, that was our problem, but with Lewis, the *intended* allegory is obvious. It sticks out of the story like the proverbial sore thumb. Malacandra (Mars) is the perfect world, performing as it should; earth is the fallen world under Satan's power. Fallen man is irrational, jealously possessive, an admirer of ugliness. His nervous desire to preserve his life becomes the self-defeating fear of death.

In *Perelandra*, two of these same men—the Christian and the instrument of the devil—engage in battle over the future of the planet Venus. Venus is also unfallen, a verdant, un-sullied Garden of Eden, peopled by two beautiful and innocent green people. In a battle to the death, Ransom, the Christian, preserves the natural innocence of the planet and its two inhabitants, assuring that Venus, at least, will not have to reenact the tumultuous history of earth, but will drift instead in a timeless, conflictless bliss, its inhabitants nestled against the benevolent bosom of nature. (One wonders whether these green folk will ever be able to "endure" the process of conceiving and rearing children, though one is led to assume they will.)

Again, on one level this story deals with a traditional sf theme. But the complexity of man's encounter with a sinless planet, which is developed so beautifully by James Blish in his *A Case of Conscience*, is completely avoided by Lewis. The idea, presumably, is that never to have fallen is equivalent to redemption.

The third volume, *That Hideous Strength*, is by far the most interesting in the trilogy and it is highly recommended to the readers, not as theology, but as a good story. This time we are back on earth and the clash between the forces of the Bent One and of Good is nearing a climax. The evil ones have built their "Tower of Babel" which will enable them to play God—a huge government-endowed scientific-military research center whose power is becoming greater than that of the government itself. The "head" of the center is . . . a head —a disembodied head whose brain is kept alive by an elaborate complex of tubes and wires. The secret goal of the center is to seize absolute power so that it can rule the earth for its own sinister purposes, purposes which (we are led to believe) would ultimately destroy all life by covering the planet with concrete and polluting all the air and water.

Meanwhile, the forces of Good are collecting themselves in a pleasant little country cottage under the direction of the same Ransom of *Perelandra* fame. Except for Ransom, the Good are a rather bumbling, emotional, well-meaning lot. Ransom has reached an ethereal, semispirit (Christlike?) state; he can inspire all who meet him with adoration. They are joined in their finally victorious "battle" by a resurrected

Merlin, who represents the morally neutral natural man, and Venus, representing the best of pre-Christian religion. The books end with an erotic, but very monogamous and proper, love-in, with husbands and wives retiring to their respective bedrooms (leaving the single folk rather at loose ends).

To give Lewis his due, he has constructed an amusing and instructive fable for our times with some insightful comment on society and human relationships. For the purposes of this study, however, we shall examine more closely his views of man and the nature of evil.

Lewis's society on Mars is peopled by creatures which suggest a good deal about the author's conception of man. The three groups suggest elements or parts within man; out of these parts come certain characteristics which are Good. Such a conception of man is a bit arbitrary; it ignores the possibility that man is an indivisible unity, not to mention the insight of psychoanalysis that man's strengths and weaknesses may be one and the same, that the strongest positive characteristics carry with them the strongest negative possibilities. While Lewis makes no moral distinction between the intellectual, the aesthetic, and the physically active, he makes precise distinctions concerning these faculties, with a premium on docility and resignation and an attitude of condescension toward aggression and rebellion.

In *Perelandra*, Lewis casts further light on his view of man. The hero, Ransom, is treated by the author (unconsciously perhaps) as a lovable but rather dumb child. He does the same with the good folk in *That Hideous Strength*— Ransom having attained a certain stature. The evil antagonist, Weston, is often compared to a nasty little boy. His "naughtiness" is epitomized by his cruel teasing and senseless torture of animals. It seems that Lewis regards men from the viewpoint of a nineteenth-century British nursery. Abstract allegory tends here to remove traces of depth or complexity; what is left tends to be devoid of constructive meaning.

The people who run Lewis's Tower of Babel have none of the complexity one finds in the usual sf scientist; therefore it is difficult to take the evil they represent very seriously. They all seem to verge on utter madness and their intellectual circumlocutions tend to amount to rank stupidity. The height of evil is summed up in the nightmarish vision of a disembodied head and the perversions of the sadistic, lesbian police chieftess. The good people are all very lovable (if at times a little weak), docile, and always polite. They are people about whom a child would feel comfortable. The evil are just plain nasty—the kind of people children are warned against in the vague hints of grown-ups.

Oh, the irony that such straight sf writers as Sturgeon, Blish, and even Heinlein would have a more profound understanding of evil than the confessing theologian! The greater irony still if Lewis turned out to be right!

There can be no doubt, however, that Lewis, for all his primness and tendency to abstraction, introduces a valuable dimension into the discussion by insisting that there is a reason for man's ill nature. But this sad state is hardly cured by the assumption that a perfect world is based upon hierarchical principles. It almost amounts to a medieval concept of "know your place"; or perhaps it's an English gentleman's view of good and bad.

A Dostoevskian Diversion

Doubtless there is need for the restoration in human consciousness of an aristocratic principle—some means of calling attention to the fact that the closed system that man likes to erect for himself is *penetrated*, pierced by what theologians have referred to as "the transcendent" or the "holy." But old social and metaphysical formulas will not help to move beyond the deep insights into man's nature that have been developed by modern psychology and existentialism. The discovery of relativity forces us to understand that any penetrating principle of unity or transcendence will be *dynamic* rather than static. Our problem in the future will be to recognize that a dynamic conception of man and God is reconcilable, even consistent with, past understandings. For biblical scholars, the move from static to dynamic categories will be recognized as a move backward as well as forward. The biblical Jehovah, who at times is pictured as eternal and absolute, is also a verbal breath of life—the *ruach Yahweh*, restless, intrusive, creative.

Dostoevsky's underground man, however malevolent, also rings more truly to our ears than the static man of Lewis. Dostoevsky suggests that if there is an image of God, however tarnished, in man, it will not be susceptible to easy categorization.

> Now I ask you: what can be expected of man since he is a being endowed with such strange qualities? Shower upon him every earthly blessing, drown him in a sea of happiness . . . ; give him economic prosperity, such that he should have nothing else to do but sleep, eat cakes and busy himself with the continuation of his species, and even then out of sheer ingratitude, sheer spite, man would play you some nasty trick. . . . simply to introduce into all this positive good sense his fatal fantastic element. . . . And that is not all: even if man really were nothing but a piano-key, even if this were proved to him by natural science and mathe-

matics, even then he would not become reasonable . . .
He will launch a curse . . . (it is his privilege, the
primary distinction between him and other animals)
it may be by his curse alone he will attain his object—
that is, convince himself that he is a man and not a
piano-key![10]

Lewis's static conception denies man precisely that element of cantankerous freedom which is the essence of humanity, a freedom which is more important to man than luxury or reason or security. Science fiction, as it deals with man, comes continually to this question, for essentially what is involved is not merely man's right to dissent, but his basic condition, which society, ultimately, is deemed powerless to change. If it is this element of perversity in man's character that "saves" him from being automated by society, how is it possible to accept a static conception of human nature as the norm? Science fiction—a great deal of it—moves consciously or unconsciously to this fundamental issue: Man's freedom to "sin" is the essence of his possibility of fulfillment and redemption. Heinlein wants to preserve this freedom for the strong—for those who can "bear" it. Lewis ascribes so much influence to the Prince of Darkness that man's fulfillment seems less related to what he does than how he is made to behave.

Anthony Burgess's A Clockwork Orange carries the question further, "redeeming" the depraved young hero in terms of a Dostoevsky-type freedom—only there is no hope held out that the redemption will result in anything but resumption of the original depravity. This suggests, possibly, that redemption and freedom are by no means the same thing, that freedom is the condition which must precede the sense of salvation.

The universe which C. S. Lewis gives us is, with minor

adjustments, the formal world of Anglican orthodoxy. Fallen man is in thrall to the forces of evil which keep him from realizing himself. However, Lewis is weak at the point of redemption precisely because his understanding of evil and of man is lacking in dynamism and complexity. He fails to see that *redemption can never be the same thing as unfallen innocence.*

Managers and Rebels

What manner of men are we? Two dominant and interrelated characteristics have emerged in our discussion. First, we are those whose desire is to control, to rationalize, to create a society or personal existence which can be understood and managed. For some, this is something which can be attained through the proper use of our own will and intelligence. For others, this new order must come from some outside intervention, such as an evolutionary leap or benevolent aliens who will impose it. To some, this order is necessary for survival or salvation. To others, the result would be the totalitarian existence of *1984* or *Brave New World.* Second, we are those who rebel against all efforts to be manipulated; we have an instinctive mistrust of "final solutions" or promised perfection. To some, this rebelliousness is our saving grace, the essence of freedom; to others, it is the source of our damnation. In any case, man can be seen as being at the center of a dynamic polarity between the desire for "law and order" and the urge to be free and spontaneous. However, whether to manage or to escape management, man is an *actor*, a dynamic integrated whole. It is only in the context of his action that these concepts take on meaning. Man cannot be conceived of in terms of static categories.

What does it mean to be human? Man may reason. Man

may intuit. Man may love. But words are hardly sufficient to encompass his potential, for he can always find new ways to put these things together. We return to the notion of *story* and of man as *actor*; we define him less in terms of capacity than of activity, of experience, of involvement; of authenticity. It is less significant that man *can* make tools, than that he *does* so. That he *does* use fire. That he *does* tell tales. That he *does* apprehend holiness, beauty, love, and, occasionally, one another. Man is the actor and seeker, and there is no limit to his ingenuity, no limit, that is, that is helpful in defining him. Even the notion of finitude, of limitation upon human capacity, that some theology has used to suggest man's nature, becomes distorted if it suggests a static state of impotence. Properly understood, both self-transcendence and finitude are themselves dynamic. Self-transcendence is *freedom to see beyond.* Finitude is the *acknowledgment of objective limitations* on man's activity.

Man as actor, as doer, operates from a complex of motives, and there is no necessary correlation between motivation and the result of action. What we sometimes regard as human "progress" may be traced as much to hate as to love, to fear as to the desire for pleasure, and may prove no progress at all. And the dominant word that comes to mind is morally neutral: curiosity. We suspect that the key to humanness lies somewhere within the conglomerate of curiosity, irrationality, inventiveness, and unpredictability. Is it also a key to hope?

Science fiction can help disorient us from present solutions and mind-sets, thus moving us a bit closer to the hope that lies in our desire to act as we must to conquer the challenges of life, whether these challenges be to tear down or to build up.

If we conceive of man primarily as actor, there is no

possible way to endow him with the right or even capacity to pass ultimate judgments. There are no static standards to which he may point in self-defense. There is no final authority in the world. And yet he acts in relation to standards beyond him. In the story certain events carry absolutes, and in that sense the antinomy between absolutism and relativism is resolved. And, indeed, the possibility of a dynamic reality in and beyond man is reasserted—if we meet him again as the actor he is.

NATURE:
dynamism and change

4

> Far from seeing in man the irrevocable and
> and unsurpassable image of God, I assert—
> more modestly and, I believe, in greater
> awe of the Creation and its infinite possi-
> bilities—that the long-sought missing link
> between animals and the really humane
> being is ourselves!
>
> —KONRAD LORENZ[1]

Science has blown the lid off nature, making it limitless—
as limitless as the edge of the universe, perhaps limitless
beyond that. It has shown dynamism and change to be aspects
of creation, even as it has exposed the tendency of matter
toward random disorder (entropy). And we are learning from
men like Konrad Lorenz how difficult it is to carve out a
humane identity for ourselves within this limitless nature.
Now we shall focus on the attitude toward nature that we
find in at least some science fiction.

If we consider the simplest and most traditional vision
of nature it is clear that the pressures man feels in the
personal and social realm can hardly be divorced from nature.
Only now has urban industrial man become aware of his
great dependence on this traditional sort of nature—on the
green fields, hills, brooks, trees, and all the other rural mani-

festations that have been crowded out of the great cities. The United States is a living parable of the mutual impotence of neglected nature and the neglected metropolis. Nature loses its value to man as attempts at human management involve the unthinking rape of its resources. The metropolis tends toward chaos as it increases in size. And in the loss of a dynamic relationship between city and country, much human malaise can be located. At the same time, the relationship still exists, like an unhappy marriage, and the effects of the separation will be felt even if the divorce appears complete.

The desecration of nature is resulting in a vast confluence of polluted water, unbreathable air, and creeping garbage gone wild. The indestructibility of plastic is a perverse index of modern technology's poor relationship with nature: you throw it away but it never disappears. Perhaps we can learn to control and direct nature for purposes that do not hamper man's drive toward liberty. Perhaps we can learn when to leave it alone. At the moment, even as nature becomes more and more the object of man's probing, it bears the brunt of his neglect.

Nature Expanded

Science fiction stretches our mind when we consider nature, for it reminds us that nature is more than green fields and trees. It assists the layman in his perception of the thin band of habitability that is the earth's biosphere. It calls attention to the potentially hostile activity of nature. If we feel ourselves "cut off from nature" in our urban environment, we must remember that we are part of it—cellular, evolved once-animal we.

Space travel in science fiction provides the most obvious avenue to an expanded perception of nature, both in terms of distance and of the visions of very different natural environments. Building on Einstein, science fiction plays on the theme of the transferability of energy and matter, the possibilities of other dimensions, other space-time complexes. In this study, we shall not discuss these themes, except to point' them out. We stand today on the threshold of a massive infusion of new knowledge which science fiction helps us to prepare for, and it may be that the Wordsworths of the future will write their sonnets in praise of yet unseen glories on unknown planets in unknown solar systems.

As we shall see even in this brief study, science fiction leaves the riddle of nature intact. If there is some agreement about man—at least about his problem—there is scant consensus about the nature . . . of nature. Is nature matter? Energy? Space? Is it benign? Indifferent? Malevolent? Can we define it for discussion purposes as *the object which human consciousness encounters,* therefore as separate from consciousness if not from cellular man? This raises all kinds of philosophical problems. Is there an immutable order beyond the flux that we detect? To what extent can science contribute to a definition of nature if science is engaged, primarily, in the formation of hypotheses rather than fixed laws? One should not feel discouraged by all these questions, for nature has always been hard to define. Philosophers, theologians, and scientists alike have pondered its mystery, plumbed its depths, and left us wondering . . .

Arthur Clarke vs. Matter

It is interesting that one of the best-known science fiction writers, long a prophet of space travel and its implications, should espouse a fundamentally negative conception of nature, insofar as nature can be identified with matter. But such seems to be the case with Arthur C. Clarke, author of *2001: A Space Odyssey*, *Childhood's End*, and a spate of other fascinating inquiries into the world of science and the future. In *Childhood's End*, alien space creatures establish a benevolent dictatorship on earth, just as man is about to penetrate outer space. Poverty, war, ignorance, and disease are eliminated; there is even an attempt to erase the resulting boredom by the development of universal education and participation in the arts. Only one basic restriction is placed on man: He is barred from research in the field of parapsychology.

The golden age is disrupted when a young child begins having dreams during which his mind leaves his body and travels to distant planets. Other children begin to have similar experiences. The wandering child-minds develop the capacity to manipulate matter. Then, as more children are affected, the minds begin to merge beyond the bodies. After a period of playing with their/its newfound power, the common mind leaves the earth, destroying it in the process. It ascends into the heavens to merge with an "overmind" which has infinite capacities to travel and manipulate matter. Man has ceased to exist. The creatures who arrived to rule the earth turn out to be the midwives of the "overmind," sent to earth to save man from self-destruction before the "birth" of the new form, and to keep him from aborting the birth of the children's common mind by stemming his advances in parapsychology. Salvation is attained in Clarke's novel by an elaborate process by which man is delivered from the tyranny of matter.

In the novel *2001: A Space Odyssey*—which Clarke published after his collaboration with Stanley Kubrick on the screenplay of the film—Clarke again introduces a free-floating mind. It is the power which intervenes at various points of human history and which lies behind the release of the astronaut at the book's end. In *2001*, the released mind seems to retain units of individual consciousness, but otherwise there is no change in Clarke's attitude toward matter:

> In their ceaseless experimenting, they [units of consciousness within the mind] had learned to store knowledge in the structure of space itself, and to preserve their thoughts for eternity in frozen lattices of light. They could become creatures of radiation, free at last from the tyranny of matter.
>
> Into pure energy, therefore, they presently transformed themselves . . .[2]

What we have here is not new to the history of metaphysical speculation and insight. It dovetails very neatly with the concept of the levels of consciousness found in the metaphysics which undergirds the shadowy world of spiritualism. But its roots are found also in the school of Christian Platonism, with its emphasis on the release of the eternal soul from the evil body. The transformation of matter into energy provides a seemingly scientific basis for such conjecture. The Greek strand of thought found in Platonism—a body-soul dualism—penetrates certain forms of Christian mysticism and has affinities with some manifestations of Eastern philosophy. Such a tendency toward the separation of mind and matter has obvious appeal. The separation is helpful in explaining evil, for its suggests that the mind is trapped in the body. If only it were free, evil would be overcome. Such an analysis is certainly therapeutic for the person caught in the vise of serious illness, for the body then becomes something to escape.

There are, however, obvious dangers inherent in such a

diagnosis. The objectification of evil in matter can lead to a disregard of the natural environment, the consequent increase of sickness, and the encouragement of escapism and a distortion of truth in our perception of reality. Opposed to the tendency to negate nature, or matter, is the whole weight of Hebrew-Christian thinking, which emphasizes the inseparability of mind and body and stresses the symbol of resurrection (a concept related to justice) in contrast to the eternity of the soul and its eventual merging with the Godhead. The Bible constantly bears witness to the fact that one cannot separate man, nature, and history in the effort to perceive meaning.

Another problem with *Childhood's End* and *2001*, if taken as possible sources of metaphysical speculation, is that individual freedom and self-consciousness are components which are devalued, and man is made subject to forces which he can neither comprehend nor control. Mind is all; it functions in a predetermined manner; it is finally a mere atom in the vague mass of "overmind."

A Treaty with Nature

If nature (matter) is seen as evil in a portion of science fiction, exactly the opposite view is present in another portion. In this view, nature is benevolent, even omnipotent, an object of reverence and respect. The source of man's problem is not his captivity within matter but his failure to live in accordance with the "natural flow." This comes through to some extent in C. S. Lewis—especially in *Perelandra*. But an extreme statement of the position is found in the story "Sea Home" by William Lee (*The Magazine of Fantasy and Science Fiction*, June 1965). A group of scientists testing out an undersea dwelling find themselves developing rapidly the physiology needed for survival in the deeps. Their mental capacity increases; they become able to absorb oxygen without conventional breathing. Their bodies adjust to the cold temperature. Eventually they opt to live out their lives more fully as sea creatures rather than return to the cramped world of "civilization."

This story suggests that it was our departure from the sea—our evolutionary move from the amphibian state—that created our problems. The Fall, in this reading, took place when we left the primordial slime. Eden was wet. Obviously Lee does not wish to impose a new fundamentalism upon us. What he calls to our attention is the need for a new treaty with nature, a cessation of the war that man has waged through either sins of omission or sins of commission; it reminds us of the pressures and strains we have put on our bodies with each advance of evolution and civilization.

Arnold Toynbee has pointed out a direct correlation between human violence in history and man's separation from nature. Not merely man's depredation of nature, but also his psychological dependency upon it, is at issue. The interrelation between man, nature, and history is revealed once again. How effective will today's social studies and reports on major "problems" be if they do not consider the dimension of nature, whether in terms of the need for a complementary relationship between city and country or of adequate air to breathe? All of man's social solutions will come to naught unless they possess an ecological dimension. How much of what sort of noise can the human ear stand? How small is the space which man can occupy without going mad? How bad must traffic become before man voluntarily crashes his cars to recall his humanity?

Here nature emerges not as the implacable enemy, something to be overcome or escaped from, but as a potential friend, willing to cooperate if only man will pay attention to its rules. Science is dependent on such a view; it is dedicated to the discernment of nature.

This positive evaluation of nature should not lead to sentimentality. Just as Christian Science makes the mistake of absolutizing the capacity of mind to overcome matter, such nature-respecting practices as natural childbirth and karate can when sentimentalized or absolutized lead to a false assumption that nature is eternally benevolent, if man but follows its laws. To sentimentalize nature is to ignore its harshness and cruelty, the price perhaps of its own mysterious evolution. Of course, the elevation of nature to a pinnacle of omnipotence returns man to the nature worship of his ancestors in which all things—evil and good—flow from the inexplicable conduct of nature. In our time this primitive mode of worship found its expression in the demonic naturalism of the Third Reich; Hitler's simplistic but appealing philosophy owed its life to the readiness of people to accept themselves as pinnacles of the natural order; like lions they became Kings of Beasts, acting toward man with more bestiality than can be attributed to the lion.

The Cry for Help

A fascinating story by Hayden Howard adds further insight to the problem of relating man and nature. In Howard's "Beyond Words," there is a small revolt against civilization. Three students, two boys and a girl, decide, in the year 1984, to go into the desert and to suspend by a mutual pact *all* use of words. During the time one of the boys is caught in a rock slide. His urgent "Help!" is the first word to break the silence. But because of unconscious jealousy and a conscious fleeing from the word "Help!" the other boy allows him to die. For this survivor, you see, "Help!" is "the word which launched civilization."[3] Thus the corrupt civilization which the three seek to escape is, by implication, the only arena in which life might be saved.

On one level the story exhibits an extreme view of the hippie-digger philosophy, the version which rejects society and moves "back to nature," which says—as one of its representatives once said to us—"The earth is good, the world is bad." There is a danger inherent in this philosophy found in the tendency to reduce the scope of what is needed to achieve the very justice and love that one sees lacking in society. The welcome optimism of the Beatles' slogan "All You Need Is Love" does not obscure the fact that love needs power and justice at its side if it is to become operative. But there is also an obvious appeal in tuning in to the natural rhythms and processes, reducing life to the very basics of survival and personal relationships.

The main thrust of Howard's story, however, is the idea that civilization begins with the cry for help. The word "help" issued in a new consciousness—the consciousness of civilizing man, man in community, man related to other men for the sake of common protection against outside danger. But if this is so, a certain choice is implied, for inherent in the word "help" is the suggestion of the other's freedom to accept or reject the cry. With the hearing of this cry and the response to it, a separation from nature takes place, and the individuality whose essence is freedom is created. Man becomes actor, becomes himself, when language gives him the means of deciding between good and evil. Before this "fall," before the establishing of civilization, the creatures we call men would have possessed freedom only insofar as animals possess it—the freedom to act by instinct alone, the freedom to scratch when they itch. The Genesis story of man's fall is directly related to man's attainment of the knowledge of good and evil, his "becoming as the gods." And it makes clear that the fall contains both a curse and a blessing. The curse is echoed in Sartre's modern dictum "Hell is other people." It is hard to live in community. It is difficult to respond to the cry for help. The blessing is the attainment of consciousness which may be advanced as a distinction between men and animals. The blessing gives rise to the curse and the curse to the blessing. The separation from nature, the attainment of consciousness, makes love possible, and that is a blessing. But the separation from nature also results in distortions, in man's attempt to create "civilizations" as though his relationship to nature were not a thing to be considered. The story of the Tower of Babel in the book of Genesis—in which God confuses language and destroys the effort of man to build a spire which will reach to the heavens—may actually be a parable of man's precipitous attempt to divorce himself from nature with more and more complex civilizations.

If this line of reasoning is correct, one can see the inadequacy of the thought of C. S. Lewis. Patently, Lewis seems to desire a return of man to the state of instinctive docility which he imagines Eden to be. But this can hardly be the destiny of man.

The blessing and the curse of the fall give rise to another observation. In the Genesis story, when Adam and Eve are cast from the Garden, God gives them garments as well as fertility. The garments are a token that he will be with them as they make the long journey of freedom toward their goal which, in biblical terms, is the universal reign of love and justice. Today we are hesitant to criticize the new vogue that is being given in some quarters to nudity. However much the display of nudity in magazines and on record jackets may have the salutary effect of making us aware of our own stuffiness, we can see here a distortion of perception, an attempt to move back to Eden rather than forward to some ultimate destiny. The conferring of fertility upon Adam and Eve suggests that God is hardly opposed to sex. The fact that fertility results in a line of descendants, moving forward in time, implies that what God does *not* desire is a return to Eden. On the musical scene, we find Bob Dylan's poetic analysis of Eden and his statement, in context, that "life is not a joke" more redemptive and hopeful than the Beatles' utterance in their context that love is "all you need." Even Robert Heinlein moves from the nudity of the nests in *Stranger in a Strange Land* to the relatively decorous deportment of the line family in *The Moon Is a Harsh Mistress*.

In modern times Dostoevsky is one who understands the freedom which is man's curse and blessing. And his notion of redemption is explicit: ultimately man must "kiss the earth." He must overcome the breach between himself and nature by an act of love that could only be generated by the blessing and curse inherent in the fall toward freedom; he cannot overcome it by denying that the fall has occurred, or by neglecting either the curse or the blessing.

Nature and Reality

Thus far the problems of nature that we have discussed are hardly new. But what happens when we move beyond the possibility of ecological disaster in the near future to the far future where imagination swings freely in space, and nature becomes something quite different from what we believe it to be? There are many stories which involve another planet or universe where the physical "laws" we hold as constants are cast aside for a new set of constants. Thomas Disch, in the novel echo round his bones, explores one such possibility right here on earth. In echo round his bones, Disch simplifies future space travel by inventing an instantaneous transmitter of matter . . . including human beings. The transmitter automatically produces a shadowy duplicate of the matter that is transferred. It finally becomes possible to produce an echo world which renders humanity invulnerable to attack. After the machine transmits a man, the remaining copy becomes an echo of the original rather than an exact duplicate. Thus, though they are the same person, the echo and the original have differing consciousnesses because of the subsequent differing history of experiences. For example, the hero's echo finds civil disobedience against the military authorities wholly acceptable, while the orginal hero cannot resolve this ethical dilemma.

If consciousness of good and evil is distinctively human, the book entertains the possibility—suggested in physical terms—that there can be more than one consciousness in each man, simultaneously or successively, as the case may be. Is a system of physics (or metaphysics in the case of Arthur Clarke) possible in which there are "progressive levels of reality, and matter can exist at each level"[4]? It is not necessary to have an answer, but the possibility is intriguing for many reasons.

One implication of the novel is a confirmation of the notion that man defines himself in his actions, and that these actions are in turn molded, at least in part, by his relationship to nature, however he may encounter it. Not only can we carry within us numerous potentialities, but we can become different persons without sacrificing our original identity. In *echo round his bones* it is not so much man's relationship to nature that is probed as the fact that nature may well have unexpected capacities related directly to the ultimate fate of man.

We can go even further into this idea of the unity of man and nature. Nature, the environment, the objective reality, helps to determine what man is to become. This can be seen both in terms of the evolution of the species and in the development of the individual. But there is in this as in other of the new science fiction the reverse cause-and-effect relationship that in some sense man "molds" nature with his consciousness, thus having a hand in determining the basic reality with which he is forced to deal. Nature then becomes, in some sense, relative and subjective. Primitive man, medieval man, Newtonian man, Einsteinian man, all endowed nature with certain characteristics which have had to be dealt with in the context of experience. And all of these understandings contained *elements of truth*, also in the context of experience. What, then, if new discoveries and world views bring to nature some reality at which, at present, we can't begin to guess? Nature, like man, must be viewed as dynamic, and the relationship between the two dynamic.

Summary and Direction

We began this study by outlining something of the apocalyptic sense of the present day, a sense rooted in the evident failure of various efforts at internal reform. We moved to an examination of man in science fiction and determined both the difficulty of arriving at a static definition and the possibility that the freedom to sin might be essential to the attainment of fulfillment. In terms of the present moment in history, we suggested that man was to be found in the tension between the desire to manage and the desire to avoid being managed. Turning to the treatment of nature in science fiction, we suggested that neither a mind-matter split with a low valuation of nature or science nor the tendency to turn nature into a god was helpful in grasping the reality which nature suggests. Nature emerges most convincingly for us as an ambiguous but possibly friendly environment. In addition, nature and man, though separated in the process of man's attainment of freedom in the course of evolution, are mutually dependent and any "redemption" of man involves full reconciliation with the dynamics of nature.

It is impossible to follow such an argument for long without recognizing that the arena in which man and nature take on their most valid meaning is history. For if we reject a return to Eden we are impelled toward an unknown future in time or beyond it. And it is precisely in the realm of history that science fiction makes its most helpful contribution to the discussion.

HISTORY:
consciousness and
the fullness of time

5

And that distill'd by magic sleights
Shall raise such artificial sprites
As by the strength of their illusion
Shall draw him on to his confusion:
He shall spurn fate, scorn death, and bear
His hopes 'bove wisdom, grace, and fear;
And you all know security
Is mortals' chiefest enemy.
—SHAKESPEARE, *Macbeth* (III. v)

History risks becoming the whipping boy of a new generation of young persons, discouraged by what they read of the past and sensing that the West offers no spiritual resources for the future. Symbolic of this is a distrust of the old which one finds carried to its logical extreme in a film such as *Wild in the Streets*. Here the teen generation takes over the political system and incarcerates persons over thirty-five, only to be confronted by the possibility of a comparable revolt by children. However fantastic this may seem on the wide screen, one need only stand close to the young to detect within some an undercurrent of hostility which, however justified in its moral indictment, could under some circumstances turn into a less than moral response. This wild scenario is less likely than the gradual disaffiliation of youth from the present social order. That momentum is so advanced in Western society as to render fatuous all easy notions of accommodation.

Science turns many youth off because of its corrupt appropriation by military power. The senseless research in germ warfare is a case in point for those who do not sense the nature of the crimes that have been committed against women and children in Vietnam—by all four sides.

Democracy turns them off because they feel powerless to exert meaningful change by means of votes.

In the search for some meaningful platform on which to stand, some youth are drawing strength from mysticism and Eastern religion, in other words, from thought patterns which are fundamentally ahistorical. Mysticism concentrates on the individual and his relation to the unchanging God, drawing one away from the ambiguities of action toward the rigors and rewards of contemplation. Certain forms of Eastern religion— and here one would have to be specific to sustain more than a passing point—tend to regard history as a circle which turns continually back upon itself, and over which man has no control. Escape from history, whether into nature or beyond nature, becomes one dominant mark of salvation. (It is unfortunate that, at a time when Western man seems occupied with the possibilities of worship, the institutional churches seem unable to move beyond patterns so identified with the culture as to become part of what the critical man wants to escape.)

As a historical religion, Christianity is concerned with what has happened, what is happening, and what will happen. But the tendency of the churches has been to avoid being iconoclastic commentators and symbolic actors in history—in imitation of Jesus. There are voids, perhaps, left by the churches' performance that help explain the turn to the non-

Western philosophies and attitudes, but one suspects that the West is genetically coded in such a way that an anti-historical jag must turn into a new historical jig or limp into limbo.

On the other hand, a valid argument against history is man's distortion of it—for example, the tendency in the West (until recently) to write history as a simplistic chronicle of the white man's progress. But despite this criticism, the answer is to be found not in escaping history but in reconstructing it as truthfully as possible, remembering, as science fiction makes us aware, that history contains past, present, and future.

Imagine a coin. On one side is space, on the other, time. Encircling it on the narrow rim is human consciousness. This is a way of suggesting the interrelationship between man, nature, and history. Man's consciousness embraces what is perceived of nature (or space) and history (or time), and that perception constitutes human knowledge. The circle of consciousness is pushed, nudged. In precarious balance the coin begins to roll. If the coin flops on either side and ceases its motion, a conclusion may be drawn. If it rolls into someone's hand, another conclusion may be drawn. There are varieties of possibilities, but if one accepts the coin as an apt analogy of an actual relationship, history can hardly be ignored.

How then is time or history perceived by the writers of science fiction? We shall focus upon the remarkable work of three authors: Walter M. Miller, Jr., Isaac Asimov, and J. G. Ballard. The choice is a bit arbitrary, for it is about the nature of history—about its enduring problems—that authors like Blish, Heinlein, and many others have much to say.

As a mind-stretching preliminary though, consider John C. Campbell's 1935 story "Night," about an astronaut cast into an indescribably distant future. All the suns in the galaxy are dead. Machines that succeeded man on earth, machines constructed to run "forever," possess only enough power to enable the astronaut to broadcast a weak radio beam to a planet where post-us robots conduct a rescue.

"A thousand ages in Thy sight are like an evening gone," goes the hymn. Today we can look back perhaps 500,000,000 years to imagine a world when, according to paleontological evidence, life on this planet became sufficiently complex to have a beginning and an end. "Time" preceded that time, and before that there were probably other suns shedding their illuminations through space. And before that there was probably something which can be called creation of some physically recognizable substance. And before that? Void? The slow death of another universe? The physical end of our world— of our universe—is probably a long time off. And it will probably end in coldness and quiet. But what then? Will a new universe arise out of the ashes? Or will that be the End? "Time, like an ever-rolling stream, bears all its sons [suns] away." Is it a circle? Or a progression with a beginning and and an end? Only time can tell.

Science fiction can stretch our imagination almost indefinitely when time is considered, but for our purposes we shall consider the aspect of time which depends upon human consciousness—human history.

The Canticle

No single sf book which deals with history is more filled with interest than A Canticle for Leibowitz by Walter M. Miller, Jr. It looks forward in three stages. The setting is an obscure monastery in the United States. The events prior to the Old Testament–style chronicle's beginning are described as follows:

It was said that God, in order to test mankind which had become swelled with pride as in the time of Noah, had commanded the wise men of that age, among them the Blessed Leibowitz, to devise great engines of war such as had never before been upon the Earth, weapons of such might that they contained the very fires of Hell, and that God had suffered these magi to place the weapons in the hands of princes . . . and there followed the Flame Deluge.[1]

Miller describes the holocaust and subsequent chaos. After the initial horror comes a period of reaction called the "Simplification," during which the learned men are killed and books are burned: "Nothing had been so hateful in the sight of these mobs as the man of learning, at first because they had served the princes, but then later because they refused to join in the bloodletting . . ." (p. 67).

Miller's learned find refuge in monasteries; only a few survive. Isaac Leibowitz (a former nuclear physicist) founds a monastic order for the purpose of preserving history. Over a period of six centuries the monks in the order gradually lose virtually everything but the symbolic structure of the knowledge that they have copied mechanically and laboriously over the years. A full thousand years after the Simplification, the world's social structure has evolved enough to become tribal again, and the tribes are continually at war. Simultaneously, as though the two are inevitable fellows, scientific knowledge begins to reassert its primacy. Men are beginning to reconstruct the meaning of the old documents. Science is revived. A "revolution" in knowledge is anticipated. "And how will this come to pass? . . . It will come to pass by violence and upheaval, by flame and by fury, for no change comes calmly over the world" (p. 206). So speaks the leading scientist of the time; but is it the inevitable truth, or does he wash his hands of consequences he might prevent?

An odd old hermit named Benjamin keeps appearing in the book. It is never clear whether he is a mutant who has survived the centuries or a symbolic incarnation of the "Wandering Jew"—perhaps the blessed Leibowitz himself. He is always looking for something, or waiting; clearly the search for the Messiah is implied.

The final section of the book thrusts us still more centuries ahead. Space ships have now been sent to colonize the planets; atomic weapons are again in the hands of men. And the church, anticipating the worst, has prepared a ship which will carry orphans, monks, nuns, and the memorabilia. This remnant is told: "Some of you, or those to come after you, will be mendicants and wanderers, teaching the chronicles of Earth and the canticles of the Crucified . . ." (p. 277). The story of man, his tragic history, his knowledge, will be perpetuated among the stars. The ship ascends as the holocaust nears.

As the flames envelop earth, the Abbot of the Order struggles with the thorny ethical problem of mercy killing, an act which his faith and intellect oppose and his emotions perhaps condone.

At the very end, the Abbot sees Mrs. Grales, a two-headed mutant—she is the head that has lived until now, the head of a cantankerous old woman. The other head is named Rachel: "It was a small head, a cherubic head, but it never opened its eyes. It gave no evidence of sharing in her breathing or her understanding" (p. 259). But now, in the hail of bombs, it is Mrs. Grales's head that is asleep, apparently dying. For the first time Rachel is awake, and the old body of Mrs. Grales begins to take on a new life and youthfulness.

It is now Rachel's body. Looking into the eyes of Rachel for the first time, the Abbot sees . . . innocence. She is without sin.

Here we have an epic of time, space, and consciousness. We have a succession of Ends and Beginnings, a concept of human history which stresses the unity of judgment and redemption. Space is the locus of the action, but while redemption is glimpsed in space and time, it is only visible as a suggestion of hope for a future which is beyond the time and space of which we are presently conscious. A notion of man comes through in this story which plays upon his seemingly inevitable tendency to destroy what he creates: "The closer men came to perfecting for themselves a paradise, the more impatient they seemed to become with it, and with themselves as well. They made a garden of pleasure, and became progressively more miserable with it as it grew in richness and power and beauty . . ." (p. 274). Thus we have a suggestion of history as it has been: Man builds his house laboriously, only to bring it crashing down. But out of the holocaust the remnant survives to carry forth the story of man.

But what is the source of the folly in man? What prevents him from building a house that can endure? Miller suggests that superimposed upon man's capricious freedom—the source at once of creative action and the seeming obligation to destroy—is a failure, an incapacity, to use this freedom properly. The freedom which is attained when man attains consciousness of good and evil, when he distinguishes himself from nature and begins to build civilization, carries with it the tendency not merely to ignore nature, but also to manipulate time, that is, to fail to distinguish between the area of existence which falls within man's control and that which does not. When man is aware of the justice which is history's goal—the justice that would exist if man's freedom to choose were exercised correctly—and when he seeks to act in accordance with that justice, his life becomes authentic. But the same freedom that draws him toward justice leads to his embitterment with the space (nature) and time (history) which he is given. And this bitterness impels him either toward despair and inaction or toward an attempt to assert a control over space and time which he does not possess. He attempts to become God, and in doing so forfeits the possibility of authentic manhood. In this context, the suggestion that God alone is the Lord of history is not a summons to human slavishness and subservience, but rather to the fulfillment of man's freedom in justice and love. And how does this freedom become so distracted?

> Really . . . the evil . . . was not suffering, but the unreasoning fear of suffering. . . . Take it together with its positive equivalent, the craving for worldly security, for Eden, and you might have your "root of evil". . . *To minimize suffering and to maximize security were natural and proper ends of society and Caesar. But then they became the only ends, somehow, and the only basis of law—a perversion. Inevitably, then, in seeking only them, we found only their opposites: maximum suffering and minimum security.* [P. 312, italics added.]

It is in man's false consciousness of his situation that his difficulty lies. History moves forward but in cyclical fashion because of man's failure to allow a proper consciousness to break through the circular pattern that his false consciousness creates. The preservation of Rachel in *A Canticle for Lei-*

bowitz testifies to the fact that out of the ashes may spring new life, to the fact that the ultimate destiny of man is to attain a correct consciousness, and only this is true purity, but not the end of struggle.

How might man—while still living out his time in nature and civilization—move beyond the seeming impasse of his false consciousness? Perhaps there is a reciprocity of sorts between the forgiveness of man by God and the forgiveness of God by man. Before her last confession Mrs. Grales desires to forgive God:

> She leaned close to whisper behind her hand. "I need be giving shriv'ness to Him, as well."
>
> The priest recoiled slightly. "To Whom? I don't understand."
>
> "Shriv'ness—to Him who made me as I am," she whimpered. But then a slow smile spread her mouth. "I—I never forgave Him for it."
>
> "Forgive God? How can you—? He is just. He is Justice, He is Love. How can you say—?"
>
> Her eyes pleaded with him. "Mayn't an old tumater woman forgive Him just a little for His Justice? Afor I be asking His shriv'ness on me?" [P. 308]

As the priest dies, he understands the step that must take place if the circle of false consciousness is to be broken. He cries out: "Listen, Man, you have to give up the bitterness—'be granting shriv'ness to God,' as she'd say—before anything; before love" (p. 314, italics added).

What becomes of the Wandering Jew at the end? We do not know; but his name is now Lazarus—the one Jesus raised from the dead. Will he wander forever in search of the Messiah, a living reminder that we must wait upon the Lord, that God alone is Lord of history? On his cabin door we find written in Hebrew the biblical words which suggest the ultimate reconciliation of space, time, and consciousness: "Hear, O Israel, the Lord our God is one Lord."

How is it possible that, with so much explicit theological discussion in this book, we do not level at Miller the same literary criticism that we did at C. S. Lewis? The comment was made of Lewis that he was first and foremost presenting a theological position and only secondarily telling a story. Miller, whatever his concern for theology, is always true to the story. His characters happen to be concerned with theological questions, but when they speak they always remain within the context of the story. Thus the theological conclusions are drawn by the characters and not by the author speaking directly to the reader. The theological realities become a part of the story itself. This is not always true of Lewis. We believe that this greatly explains why the theology found in Miller as drawn by us from the story tends to be more dynamic and forceful.

The Triumph of Order

Is it possible to conceive of a future history in which the tragic cycle described by Miller might give place to the establishment of universal love and justice among men? Let us follow to its limits one of the best probes of this question within science fiction—a work of Isaac Asimov. His development of a possible future history is found in the trilogy *Foundation*. Like *Canticle*, Asimov's formidable work covers a period of 1,000 years, but the story begins many millennia hence.

As the story begins, we find that a science called psychohistory has gained ascendancy. The science operates on the assumption that history is predictable: if one deals with sufficient masses of people their actions become subject to statistically verifiable laws of chance. Psychohistory is a mathematical science as precise as physics.

We learn that there are twenty-five million inhabited planets in the galaxy, all of them loyal to an Empire with a capital city-planet called Trantor. Hari Seldon, mathematician and founder of psychohistory, has predicted that the Empire will fall within 500 years. This "treasonous" forecast results in his banishment . . . to the edge of the galaxy. Here he and his followers establish a scientific refuge to preserve human knowledge during the period of chaos following the fall of the Empire. This preserve, known as the Foundation, expects to reduce the period of chaos from 30,000 to 1,000 years.

At the other edge of the galaxy, Seldon establishes a second Foundation in the hope that the two foundations will ultimately merge to form a stronger Empire.

When the predicted chaos envelopes the galaxy, Seldon's first Foundation helps dispense technological know-how to desperate planets, eventually conquering the remains of the toppled Empire. But at this point an unanticipated figure emerges to throw Seldon's plan into seeming disarray. He is the Mule, a mutant with the capacity to work his will directly on the emotions of others. He defeats the first Foundation and seeks to locate the second Foundation. A battle follows in which the Mule is "converted" and brought under the power of the second Foundation's superior capacity to control emotions.

Finally, the second Foundation contrives a means of remaining hidden and, thus protected, proceeds to manipulate events toward the formation of a perfect society. Asimov explains:

> It is . . . a civilization based on mental science. In all the known history of Mankind, advances have been made primarily in physical technology . . . Control of self and society has been left to chance or to the vague gropings of intuitive ethical systems based on inspiration and emotion. As a result, no culture of greater stability than about fifty-five percent has ever existed, and these only as the result of great human misery.[2]

Here we have the triumph of a principle of order over a principle of freedom, based on Asimov's faith in science and the assumption that humanity holds within itself over the long haul the key to its own survival and happiness. However, in a later book, *The End of Eternity*, Asimov seems to develop some doubts about the humanistic-benevolent-control theory of ultimate fulfillment. "Eternity" is the name of an elite group of people who range time, but otherwise exert a control over human affairs similar to that of the second Foundation. The price that is paid for the smooth regulation and control of history is a civilization pervaded by mediocrity: "In ironing out the disasters of Reality, Eternity rules out the triumphs as well." Rationalization of society and control of man, no matter how enlightened, may bring a spurious form of happiness, but it limits or eliminates triumph and ecstacy. Finally, Asimov expresses hope that somehow an effective power structure will be formed which recognizes that "there are many happinesses, many goods, infinite variety . . . *That* is the Basic State of mankind."[3]

Can society bring itself out of its cycle of chaos, reconstruction, and chaos? And if it can, will the expense be worth paying? Will it not involve a sacrifice of consciousness? Dostoevsky makes a most convincing case against the humanistic solution:

I hold no brief for suffering nor for well-being either. I am standing for . . . my caprice, and for its being guaranteed to me when necessary. Suffering would be out of place in vaudevilles, for instance; I know that. In the "Palace of Crystal" it is unthinkable; suffering means doubt, negation, and what would be the good of a "palace of crystal" if there could be any doubt about it? And yet I think man will never renounce real suffering, that is, destruction and chaos. Why, suffering is the sole origin of consciousness. Though I did lay it down at the beginning that consciousness is the greatest misfortune for man, yet I know man prizes it and would not give it up for any satisfaction. Consciousness, for instance, is infinitely superior to twice two makes four.[4]

Like Miller, Asimov goes straight to the root question: How is there to be justice, fulfillment, salvation for man, given the present warped state of human consciousness? Miller answers that we can have no final guarantee that any human action will avoid suffering. We are called to cease our frantic quest for security and to reconcile ourselves with the Lord of history. There will most likely be no predictable resolution of man's freedom within history. Asimov's answer would be that man's intuitive ethic is hardly an adequate means of curtailing his tendency to aggression and self-destruction. What is needed is a scientifically applied rein upon man's evil instincts. This is possible in the future, but one must candidly admit the limitations of such an approach. Both writers have a somewhat pessimistic view of man; but both are optimistic about the capacity of time to produce a more or less hopeful end to the story.

An important issue which Asimov raises is the extent to

which history is predictable. Futurology has become a popular endeavor in advanced industrial society, whether in the astrology which anticipates the next millennium as the Aquarian age, or in the work of various research groups toward developing refinements in techniques of prediction. Naturally the effort to anticipate coming developments is an essential activity of society, concerned as it must be for its future welfare. But there is an interesting twist to the whole notion of predictability. Not a few science fiction tales deal with the ironic by-products of the ability to know in advance, for example, the time of one's death. Omniscience emerges as a mixed blessing, as Hecate suggests in the passage from Macbeth quoted at the beginning of this chapter. Predictability may be to contemporary power management (whether in Washington or Moscow) what the vote is when the political process actually provides alternatives—a means of exercising control. Thus, with predictability as well as a host of other by-products of burgeoning science, the question is, Who is in charge and what are the constraints?

Here it is hard to resist the inclusion of a portion of Aldous Huxley's introduction to an edition of *Brave New World* published fourteen years after the original appearance of the novel in 1932:

> . . . I assume that the all-powerful executive and its managers will succeed in solving the problem of permanent security. . . . To bring about [full security] we require, among others, the following discoveries and inventions. First, a greatly improved technique of suggestion—through infant conditioning and, later, with the aid of drugs . . . Second, a fully developed science of human differences, enabling government managers to assign any given individual to his or her proper place in the social and economic hierarchy.

> . . . Third . . . a substitute for alcohol and the other narcotics, something at once less harmful and more pleasure-giving than gin or heroin. And fourth . . . a foolproof system of eugenics, designed to standardize the human product and so to facilitate the task of the managers. . . . As political and economic freedom diminishes, sexual freedom tends compensatingly to increase. And the dictator . . . will do well to encourage that freedom. . . . it will help to reconcile his subjects to the servitude which is their fate.

Huxley says that government in the near future will be conducting massive inquiries into the problem of happiness, and concludes:

> Today it seems quite possible that the horror may be upon us within a single century. . . . Indeed, unless we choose to decentralize and to use applied science, not as the end to which human beings are to be made the means, but as the means to producing a race of free individuals, we have only two alternatives to choose from: either a number of national, militarized totalitarianisms, having as their root the terror of the atomic bomb and as their consequence the destruction of civilization (or, if the warfare is limited, the perpetuation of militarism); or else one supra-national totalitarianism, called into existence by the social chaos resulting from rapid technological progress in general and the atomic revolution in particular, and developing, under the need for efficiency and stability, into the welfare-tyranny . . .[5]

For many reasons, predictability and manageability of the future can be a two-edged sword. Huxley's analysis may have the possibility of incapacitating us by burdening us with a sense of despair. If what he says is true, why go on?

It may be that a more hopeful and realistic stance is one which recognizes the openness of the future. Herbert Butterfield closes his masterful *Christianity and History* with these words:

> Christians have too often tried to put the brake on things in the past, but at the critical turning-points in history they have less reason than others to be afraid that a new kind of society or civilisation will leave them with nothing to live for. . . . There are times when we can never meet the future with sufficient elasticity of mind, especially if we are locked in the contemporary systems of thought. We can do worse than remember a principle which both gives us a firm Rock and leaves us the maximum elasticity for our minds: the principle: Hold to Christ, and for the rest be totally uncommitted.[6]

A New Slant on Time

So far our discussion of history has illuminated fundamentally linear concepts of time. History is seen as a straight line, punctuated by upheavals, reaching ultimately, perhaps, some resolution of its trials and tribulations. We have looked to the future as though our sense of time were accurate, as though it were an objective reality somehow beyond us. But what happens to our understanding of history when the linear concept of time is shaken? The young English sf writer J. G. Ballard is preoccupied with time, and his novels and stories give us a new slant on it. For Ballard time assumes grotesque, dreamlike forms. Human consciousness alters the conventional notion of chronology. The paintings of Francis

Bacon—whom Ballard admires—provide a visual sense of the author's preoccupation with the psychic states that may be more "real" than any objective notion of time or history.

One Ballard story, "The Day of Forever," describes a "time" when the earth ceases to rotate on its axis. In another, "Time of Passage," a man lives his life from death to birth. Throughout Ballard's work there is a constant interplay, a switching back and forth of cause and effect, between a fault in natural time and a distortion in consciousness. Time becomes subjective, frightening, something to be escaped or by which to be absorbed.

In his Vermilion Sands stories, Ballard's characters are subjected to a totally leisure-time existence—hours filled with boredom, insanity, fear of death. Time has stopped. There is nothing beyond the pointless games that are played to relieve the pressure of boredom. Whenever one seeks to obtain one's bearings, some trick is played, as though human perception were distorted, in Ballard's words, by "some faulty junction of time and space."[7]

Ballard develops the notion of what he calls the Hubble Effect to provide a possible scientific rationale for the phenomenon he describes in *The Crystal World*. This is a process by which matter is crystallized.

> We now know that it is time . . . which is responsible for the transformation. The recent discovery of anti-matter in the universe inevitably involves the conception of anti-time as the fourth side of this negatively charged continuum. Where anti-particle and particle collide they not only destroy their physical identities, but their opposing time-values eliminate each other, subtracting from the universe another quantum from its total store of time. It is random discharges of this

type, set off by the creation of anti-galaxies in space,
which have led to the depletion of the time-store available to the materials of our own solar system.

The process of crystallization is a means of describing not
only a typically exciting sf theme, but also Ballard's subjective feelings about time:

> Just as a super-saturated solution will discharge itself
> into a crystalline mass, so the super-saturation of mat-
> ter in our continuum [of depleted time] leads to its
> appearance in a parallel spatial matrix. . . . The pro-
> cess is theoretically without end, and it may be
> possible eventually for a single atom to produce an
> infinite number of duplicates of itself and so fill the
> entire universe . . .[8]

Is Ballard projecting onto a cosmic screen, made possible
by the mathematics of physics, a sense of despair—of stopped
time—reflected in such contemporary realities as cancer, the
population explosion, the overcrowding of the city? Perhaps.
For Ballard there is only one response to the phenomenon
of crystallization: Embrace it. Thus, one of his heroes says,
"There the transfiguration of all living and inanimate forms
occurs before our eyes, the gift of immortality a direct con-
sequence of the surrender by each of us of our own physical
and temporal identities. However apostate we may be in this
world, there perforce we become apostles of the prismatic
sun" (pp. 202-203). Man gains a form of immortality—end-
less consciousness of a world of intense crystalline beauty
where *nothing ever happens*. History is not merely suspended;
it is obliterated.

What *is* time? What is its relation to the three-dimen-
sional world—to space, to nature? Can we jog ourselves back

to the linear concept of time by suggesting that Ballard is merely producing in intense metaphors a child's sense of time? Imagination is supreme; there seems no end to life. But then we are jolted by the child's vision gone terribly sour. For the normal child, the sense of the moment is thoughtless and joyful. For Ballard, it seems dictated by the overwhelming fear of death.

What, then, is this life without death for which he longs? In *African Genesis*, Robert Ardrey describes it as follows:

> Pre-Cambrian life was, I suppose, a Utopia of a sort. Non-disturbance was the motto carved on its walls. Time passed, and did not pass. Separate organisms existed, and did not exist. Lacking individuality, there was little conflict. Lacking mortality, there was no fear. Peace, that supposed desideratum of the human condition, here reigned like a fat old queen. . . . Life was good. For all those who speak persuasively concerning the collective soul . . . I can only recommend the immortal slime.[9]

Some mutation or series of mutations occurred on this planet which led to the process of reproduction rather than simple division among organisms, and an explosion of variety took place. The process of birth, life, and death entered the picture. History was born. "It would seem to me a very great question whether, had death not intervened, we should not all of us still be lost in some remote, pre-Cambrian slime. And if life is to be regarded as in its essence good, then death must be reverenced as its foremost angel" (p. 217).

Ballard's fear of death negates dynamic consciousness: "Looking out . . . this afternoon, I felt, not for the first time, that the whole landscape was compounded of illusion, the hulks of fabulous dreams drifting across it like derelict galleons."[10]

Ballard seems to suggest that the modern world, like the individual paralyzed by the fear of death, lacks the will to continue. Or that, caught between the failure of past action and the inability to conceive future action, man seeks meaning in a trancelike preoccupation with timeless beauty—an escape into a form of aesthetic, eternal psychedelia: "In the evenings Beatrice and I sit among the sonic statues, listening to their voices as the fair weather clouds rise above Coral D, waiting for a man in a dark-winged glider, perhaps painted like candy now, who will come in on the wind and carve for us images of sea horses and unicorns, dwarfs and jewels and children's faces."[11]

Ballard seems to have found his way into the depths of the great collective unconscious, only to remain stuck there, trapped among the primordial images . . . sitting, unable to take the next step. And if there is a suggestion here of escape into the ahistorical vision of an Eastern philosophy, the setting remains nevertheless unalterably Western.

In spite of our criticisms of his visions, Ballard remains for us one of the most powerful voices of contemporary science fiction. Indeed, there is real validity in symbolically stopping time so that we can momentarily cease our seemingly headlong rush into the future and take a good long look at where we are right now.

One discerns, then, at least three propositions concerning history—all of them an implicit commentary on the present crisis in Western society, each of them suggesting a possible direction or mood. We find in Ballard a diagnosis of a response to historical crisis rather than an actual concept of history. Meaning is found in the frozen moment, but a somewhat empty meaning with death hovering in the wings. In both Asimov and Miller we find the notion of history as a process which leads to some end, and in both we find a possible basis for hope if hope is seen primarily as the possibility that man can *do* or *be* something, that the consciousness whose essence is freedom is yet free and may yet have an effect. The paradox of time and eternity, of action and passivity, is solved not by some simple adjustment of perspective, but by the realization that out of the paradox springs a possibility of human realization. The very forces which illuminate our incapacity confer capacity. And the image of historical man is again asserted as that of actor: as meddler, tinkerer, rebel, helper, sufferer—defending freedom and seeking in full consciousness the fullness of time, the resurrection, the final judgment, the reign of love.

THE SHATTERED RING:
science fiction and
the quest for meaning

6

> The appearance of the wheels and their work was like unto the colour of a beryl: and they four had one likeness: and their appearance and their work was as it were a wheel in the middle of a wheel. When they went, they went upon their four sides: and they turned not when they went. As for their rings, they were so high that they were dreadful; and their rings were full of eyes round about them four. And when the living creatures went, the wheels went by them: and when the living creatures were lifted up from the earth, the wheels were lifted up. . . . As for the wheels, it was cried unto them in my hearing, O wheel.
>
> —EzEKIEL 1:16-19; 10:13, K.J.V.

From its early technological imaginings to the present day, science fiction has contributed to our understanding of the future, man, nature, and history. It has become—to use a phrase common among the writers themselves—speculative fiction,* a term which serves to broaden its scope. And, in

---

*Originated, we understand, by Robert Heinlein some thirty years ago.

recent years, it has gained a literary and artistic self-consciousness. The younger sf writers have been encouraged and supported by journals like *The Magazine of Fantasy and Science Fiction* and the excellent British *New Worlds of Science Fiction*. As a result, many have begun to take themselves more seriously as writers, as contributors to contemporary speculation. They look back to the old masters as their forerunners and teachers, but few of these men are producing today. The future of science fiction lies with a generation whose names are generally not as well known as most of those we have dealt with in this study. Among the newer writers, we have mentioned the Britishers Thomas Disch and James Ballard. Disch's recent book *Camp Concentration* is considered by some to be his best so far. Ballard is by no means as static artistically as the incredible scenes of stasis and stopped time that dominate much of his sf. His writing is as finely tuned as Sturgeon's, and his more recent work suggests that there is beauty and value in slowing things down in our chaotic time to regain a vision and a starting point in re-perceiving the world.

The American successors to Sturgeon and Heinlein, at least in the size and scope of their writings, are Samuel R. Delany and Roger Zelazny. They will be dealt with later in this chapter.

Some forty new sf books are published every month. The sheer rate of production guarantees that sf will contribute three or four volumes a year that will stand up against any literary offerings. Sometimes the exigencies of the sf marketing system make it very difficult to locate the lights among the bushels. New releases remain only a few months on the stands; years may elapse before a particularly good book is reissued. Secondhand bookstores in certain cities can be a godsend to the seeker; there are sf aficionados whose libraries are gold mines; and, as a last resort, one can always write to the publishers.

To those already named we would add R. A. Lafferty, Keith Laumer, Larry Niven, Norman Spinrad, Joanna Russ, and John Brunner as new (good) writers who have been around for a while. (One very recent novel, which we cannot categorize but which seems to bridge a gap between Wells-type questions and McLuhanesque intuitions, is Brunner's *Stand on Zanzibar*. We recommend it.) Newer writers include Dean R. Koontz, Mark Geston, Laurence Yep, Bruce McAlister, and Vance Aandahl. The list is never complete. We're sorry if we have omitted anyone's favorite.

But no list of new authors, however complete, will help us to discern the direction of science fiction, its current and future contribution to our attempt to make sense of our time and conceive a way into the future. At best, we can select some trends within the newer science fiction and offer some judgment as to where they might take us. We can, by pointing to what has impressed us, suggest where we would like sf to go.

It can be argued that the modern era has multiplied the number and complexity of external experiences and possibilities available to us: growing physical mobility, dislocating new forms of transport, traumatic confrontations with myriad environmental conditions and changes, TV. We are no longer likely to live our lives out amid relative seclusion, among a few familiar people. We shall increasingly face lives of constant dislocation, which will confuse our variously acquired orientations. Our sense of control over our immediate environment will diminish, and this could lead to frustration. This is already happening, of course. If this is so, even as politics must somehow learn to regulate external arrangements for our benefit and peace, so must art help us to order our inner senses in such a way as to enable us to deal positively with what is happening. And religion must pay more attention to the restoration of spiritual depth to the culture.

The chaos in the present world tends to confuse the various functions of art, politics, and religion. Each domain feels somehow responsible to comprehend all of life and provide a comprehensive Answer. Perhaps we will find social and personal health when politics, art, and religion are functioning in a harmoniously supplementary way: politics ordering the external world and tempering its brutalities, while leaving the person free to develop his own mode of perception of and participation in that external reality; art purifying, refining, and developing the language and visions for imaginative reflection; and religion reemerging with a dimension of truth that can provide both a moral direction (without being moralistic) and a mythological framework with excitement and inspiration, perhaps helping to bridge the realms of art and politics.

If there is value in this line of thought, the suggestion is that science fiction will be rendering its best service when it seeks to renew the realm of art, that is, when it helps us to order and comprehend our "inner space" and explore the vocabulary and visions of mythological dimensions. This is accomplished when sf writers take seriously their work as artists. That is, when they help us to see, hear, and understand.

In this context, the increased use of religious and traditional mythological motifs within sf constitutes a positive direction, a basis for the assertion that sf is moving into a special position of potential leadership within the written arts. It is to an examination of these mythological and religious elements in the exploration of inner space that we shall turn in closing this study.

In the story "The Consciousness Machine" by Josephine Saxton (*Fantasy and Science Fiction*, June 1968), we see an almost prototypal example of how one can do a mythological exploration of inner space using the scientific framework of science fiction. This is a story within a story. The machine and its use by psychologists of a future time are the framework. This framework enables us to say, "Yes, this is familiar; it is not superstition or fantasy—we are in touch with a concrete, external reality." But the consciousness machine extracts a story from the depths of one person's consciousness which is both intensely personal and of mythological dimension. The machine is ordinarily used to make sick minds well or "whole" in terms of society's definition of wholeness, much in the way psychoanalysis functions today. But when the machine is used by mistake on an already healthy person, it is found that a new definition of wholeness becomes possible. The power of an internal story breaks through to shatter the old human limits.

As a story within a story—a wheel revolving within a wheel—both stories are absolutely necessary. The external reality, the machine, and the human beings involved in historical experience make possible the development and realization of an internal artistic ordering of an internal story, which in turn can break through and turn the external reality into something new. The book of Job is of similar literary construction with an important difference. The framework, the touchstone, the outer circle, is the mythological story of an argument between God and Satan. Job's experience, his achievement of new consciousness, is the story which unfolds within that framework. The difference between these two literary constructions marks the difference between two world views, but the two circles are there, acting upon one another to shatter old limits in both circles.

We would advance the analogy that the best new science fiction functions as a sort of literary "consciousness machine." It is peculiarly adapted to help us break through our reality-oriented, "rational" world view by its combination of "science" and "fantasy" and its development of totally new environments that are plausible.

Science fiction has always served the function of what has traditionally been called folktale. Three elements within many folktales are the journey, the presence of magic (both malevolent and beneficent), and a hero who, through courage, luck, and/or the use of wit, triumphs in a strange environment. The sf folktale hero, unlike the heroes of the old myths, is an ordinary mortal, but he has a capacity to adjust to new circumstances, even thriving on them.

Throughout history, folktale and myth have been closely related, and it is not clear which preceded the other. Folktales deal with man's possibility of overcoming a drab existence with acts of courage; myths, as Michael Grant has noted in *Myths of the Greeks and Romans*, tend to have ambiguous or unhappy endings, whereas folktales represent the triumph of man against great odds. The folktale overcomes; the myth suggests ambiguities of existence that will not be resolved within the bounds of conventional consciousness and capacity. Both myth and folktale confirm the existence within consciousness of collective memory and (sometimes unconscious) striving toward a resolution in *story* of life's contradictions and disparities.

Science fiction, like the old folktales, is escapist literature, relieving drabness, boredom, or a sense of powerlessness with visions of human triumph. To this common element of folk-tale, the new sf writers (some of them) add the dimension of myth, precisely the dimension that is needed, in our view, for sf to make a significant contribution to the refurbishing of art, the quest for meaning.

Perhaps a truly redemptive story is one which combines myth and folktale, one which moves toward triumph for man without glossing over the tragic elements of existence. The pure folktale relieves boredom and the sense of powerlessness. It lifts us out of our humdrum existence and gives us a sense of new possibility. It can inspire us to go on, be open to adventure, and enjoy humor. But it cannot inspire the tragic heroism which faces the inevitability of death, and it cannot provide human consciousness with the inspiration to deal with shattering new experience. The concern with myth serves as a sign from some authors of a willingness to explore the very roots of culture, the very underlying experiences of death and rebirth, of suffering and tragedy, which must be dealt with in any literature that fulfills an artistic function. The mytho-logical dimension is nothing less than the concern for depth, truth, and meaning carried by the story. As such the presence or absence of specific references to myths is unimportant.

We shall concentrate on three examples of how stories with mythological references and dimensions emerge within the framework of fairly traditional science fiction orientation: *The Ring of Ritornel*, by Charles Harness; *Lord of Light*, by Roger Zelazny, and finally, *The Einstein Intersection*, by the author whom we regard as the brightest star in the current sf constellation, Samuel R. Delany.

Harness's *Ring of Ritornel* suffers from awkward writing and a lugubrious, intricate plot, but it occasionally reaches poetic heights and contains symbols which suggest elements of the contemporary sf quest in the direction we have been discussing. The narration is set in an incomprehensibly distant future. Earth has colonized the galaxy. While trying to suppress the inevitable rebellions of its colonies, it has touched off a massive war which has resulted in its own razing. Fearing the possible destruction of civilization in the entire galaxy, a group of scientifically acute, arachnid "humanists" devise an experiment to preserve civilization by bringing it full circle. They would do this by finding a man and a woman who are to be placed on the razed planet Earth. The planet would then be isolated in a universe of antimatter to begin the life process again. Drawing from the old Terran myth of Adam and Eve, their search is for a motherless virgin, born of a man.

The search is successful, but the final outcome is changed by the intervention of chance. The woman is human, but the man who is destined for her mate is a mutant, a winged centaur with a superhuman mind. Thus, the ring of Ritornel is shattered. (Ritornel is the name of the predestinarian, cyclical religion which the original experiment spawned.) Opposed to Ritornel (eternal return?) is a religion of chance, Alea. Ritornel and Alea are moving in continual interaction and conflict. They have become the opposing galactic gods. Here we have an imperfect but interesting attempt to give conceptual life to a very real problem in our experience—the surprising, the unexpected, the chance. In spite of its faults, it is difficult to read *The Ring of Ritornel* without coming away with a renewed way of seeing, of ordering, some of the things which happen.

We have already mentioned Roger Zelazny. In 1967 his *Lord of Light* emerged as a high point in his already well-constructed literary career, and the book is an important example of myth in science fiction, used to explore present, largely inner experiences. In the novel the Hindu pantheon is used to illuminate a conflict between those who would withhold technological know-how from a primitive, holocaust-crushed civilization (for their own good) and those who would allow the bereft civilization to proceed in a normal or even an accelerated way to technological self-realization. On this level, the story poses the moral question of the right of a group of people with advanced knowledge and at least some insight into the human predicament to regulate the choices of those with limited access to knowledge and power, i.e., to "play god." It is the age-old and thoroughly modern problem of self-determination and the proper use of power: who, if anyone, has the right to play god and under what circumstances. The hero, one of the "gods" himself, comes out on the side of violent revolution against the gods and manages to overthrow the celestial domination by mustering various superhuman forces. It is a kind of heavenly civil war which finally determines man's fate. In this sense it is very much like the tales of conflict of all primitive mythologies in which the gods intrigue and battle with each other, and where the outcome for men is incidental to the resolution of the individual god-sized ambitions and jealousies. Zelazny's hero is a rather engaging man called Sam who "never claimed to be a god. But then, he never claimed not to be a god."[1] He is never completely happy with his decision to destroy the god establishment. "He thought upon this city and these gods, and he knew of its beauty and its rightness, its ugliness and its wrongness. He thought of its splendor and its color, in contrast to that of the rest of the world, and he wept as he raged, for he knew that he could never feel either wholly right or wholly wrong in opposing it" (p. 174).

At this point one suspects that there is an iconoclastic

dimension to this story which goes beyond the mere criticism of political power elites. The beauty, awesomeness, power, oppressiveness of the gods themselves—religion itself—is called into question. Have they not had their way with man too long? Sam is a Buddha-Jesus-Mohammed figure who has appeared throughout history to call into question the god establishment. But he has never been fully successful. Nor is he successful now. After the great civil war, after the dead and debris are cleared away, after it is clear that Sam's side has won, it turns out that most of the gods are on Sam's side anyway. Some have changed their names. Some, to be sure, were killed, but new, younger gods are available to assume their places. Some have acquired new bodies. Their political hold has been destroyed for the time being and their power is scattered. But they have all retained their superior powers and access to rejuvenation. "The Lokapalas [gods] are never defeated," says one god toward the end of the book. And, one supposes, they may appear at any time with new oppressions and policies to tamper with man's attempts at shaping his own destiny. At which point, we are led to hope that Sam will appear again to fight them. A cyclical pattern is broken but not broken.

Only Vishnu remains to rule in the celestial city which he helped create. Vishnu, as Zelazny describes him, is the god of lust and revelry. Does this mean that in the reality of our present experience he is the one god capable of arousing awe and worship?

Lord of Light is a large book, and it contains undeveloped smatterings of more themes than are suggested here. Its primary importance—apart from its suggestion of man's dilemma in the face of ancient deities that he cannot quite cast from consciousness—is as an attempt to link a large and complex body of religious myth to modern concerns. Its historical, scientific, science fiction setting is assumed, normative, undercut—acting as a framework out of which the story operates, rather than as a theme to be explored. Even so, one could only conceive of the book as science fiction–new wave. If Zelazny does not suggest the lineaments of new consciousness, he performs the important artistic function of helping to clarify our remembrance of how gods operate, a distinctly mythological concern.

A somewhat different approach to the use of myth and folktale in science fiction is found in *The Einstein Intersection* by Samuel R. Delany. This book is less ambitious in complexity but more original in manipulation of the themes than *Lord of Light*. Here Delany produces a splendid probe of myth, combining snatches of modern culture, the story of Billy the Kid, the ancient myths of Theseus and Orpheus, and elements drawn from the Gospels. *Kairos!* Intersection of history with a word that releases man to act. A purification of language. An ordering of inner experience. Delany quotes John Ciardi: "A poem is a machine for making choices." As a good pre-myth, the book is impossible to summarize; one can only exclaim that Delany has helped raise up the possibility of a new beginning and that this possibility is what authentic consciousness lives by. Since summary would do injustice to the story, fragmentary notes will have to suffice.

It is after the holocaust. Lobey, the hero, loves the silent girl Friza. She is killed. He stumbles into an underground maze of old bomb shelters and defeats a contemporary minotaur. "I suppose you have to exhaust the old mazes before you can move into the new ones. It's hard."[2] So says the underground computer, PHAEDRA, who runs the abandoned underworld.

Lobey travels to the city.

Lobey must find Kid Death and kill him. But Kid Death is also looking for Lobey.

Lobey joins some dragon herders, including the two mutants, Spider ("Amber haired, four handed, and slightly hump-backed . . . seven feet of bone slipped into six feet of skin . . . And he laughed like dry leaves crushed inside his chest" [p. 63]) and Green-eye (one-eyed, mute, communicates by projecting a song inside your head).

They arrive in the city.

Spider is omnipresent.

Green-eye is crucified by a reveling mob, hung from a tree. But it is Lobey who finally deals the death blow.

It is Spider, not Lobey, who finally kills Kid Death. But for Spider to succeed, Lobey must play his flute; his music paralyzes Kid Death. He becomes Spider's necessary partner.

We do not know whether Green-eye will come down from the tree. . . . Lobey killed him; Lobey has the power to bring him back.

Near the close Lobey hears Spider say: "As we are able to retain more and more of our past, it takes us longer and longer to become old; Lobey, everything changes. The labyrinth today does not follow the same path it did at Knossos fifty thousand years ago. You may be Orpheus; you may be someone else, who dares death and succeeds. Green-eye may go to the tree this evening, hang there, rot, and never come down. The world is not the same. That's what I've been trying to tell you. It's different" (p. 119).

Lobey does not return to his original world. First he must travel another journey—explore the stars.

But it will all be waiting for Lobey when he returns.

It may all be different.

Perhaps *The Einstein Intersection* hints: There are three

elements in the creation of myth—the myths that have gone before, the poet who will sing the new myths, creating the "machines for making choices," and the appropriate historical situation. The old myths are ready. The poets are ready. Consciousness of a crucial difference exists. But the moment has not yet come. Or rather, as the author suggests in a note from his journal: "Endings to be useful must be inconclusive" (p. 125).

There is a clue: Lobey was the killer of Green-eye. He learns that he has the power to bring back to life those he has killed. Green-eye, in turn, has the power to bring Lobey's lover from Hell. This is the departure from the original Orpheus myth, the suggestion that a reconciliation can take place, making the previously impossible possible.

If The Einstein Intersection can be called a pre-myth, in that its resolution is inconclusive, perhaps it should remain so, perhaps this is an appropriate vehicle in our time. If the element of the folktale, the belief that human action can make a difference, that something can happen to break the pattern, is to remain operative, the ending cannot be written. No final ring can be inscribed to enclose, imprison, restrain. Rings can be shattered.

Where do these three books lead us in our discussion of myth as a dimension of the newer sf? There is one sense in which our preoccupation with myth involves us in conflict with our formerly stated views on history as somehow linear and purposive rather than cyclical. Walter J. Ong describes myth and mythological thinking in a perfectly valid way as follows:

> . . . archetypes and myth involve us in anhistorical or even antihistorical thinking. Archetypal thinking runs counter to some of the deepest convictions of con-

> temporary man, his persuasion of the actuality of
> history and his commitment to what is lone, unique,
> induplicable. . . . it tends to resolve actuality into a
> series of perpetual repetitions, where nothing can be
> unique at all, since everything recurs endlessly.[3]

Modern writers like Ballard have helped us to see that any
attempt to conceive of time as something separated from human
consciousness will be a distortion. Nevertheless, it is true that
myth has usually dealt with the eternal verities, the repetitious
occurrences within history—particularly the process and tragedy of individual life and death. It represents the principle
behind all religious ritual. Concern with myth can represent
a desire to get back in tune with nature, to move again with
the rhythms of the tides and seasons, accepting the astro-
logical givens as beyond our control, and not to struggle
against the seemingly inevitable. There is a sense in which
this is very good. Much of what we think of as wisdom, true
heroism, and feelings of awe spring from this posture.

We have already suggested in our chapter on nature that
nothing will be solved if we insist on cutting ourselves off
from nature and the repetitious cycles of which we are a part.
But choices still present themselves and choices are not made
for us. It is this fact, perhaps, which accounts for a certain
frustration we felt in reading Lord of Light. In spite of its
updating process and historical setting, there is an underlying
assumption—perhaps it is Zelazny's, perhaps it is built into
the body of myth he uses—that nothing really changes, that
the gods never really die or alter, that what man does is
basically irrelevant. True? Yes—but . . . This hardly does
justice to either human or divine freedom.

Actually science fiction adds a new dimension to our old

concept of myth. Committed to the future as it is, it need not rely in its future development on the repetitions of the past, on the cycles of traditional myth. For the theme of *newness*, of a future, is intrinsic to science fiction. The mutation, the holocaust, the consciousness machine, moves in to shatter the old circle. Whether one views these processes as chance, human freedom, or actions of God in history, the circle is broken; the new man, the new beginning, becomes possible. Things can be different. It is Delany who takes the traditional themes and concerns of sf and blazes a path for the future by endowing them with a capacity to illuminate the present with a refurbishing of the imagination.

It is through the work of young artists like Delany (along with new troubadours like Bob Dylan) that the hopeful consciousness is illuminated. Folktale and myth combine in a new synthesis—new unless one accepts the assertion of Christianity that myth and folktale have already coalesced to break the circle of impotence. In which case it remains for remembering consciousness to appropriate the good freedom that lies within. In which case it is possible to speak of a Second Coming and live in expectation even as we range ourselves against the distortions of nature, man, and history that authentic consciousness reveals.

Hope for the world lies in a shattering of old forms, in a reappropriation of life, first by recovering the freedom to act that is given with humanity, then by an exploratory life dedicated to the search for the fullness of time in time. The results must remain inconclusive. We have the possibility that the time of a new consciousness is at hand, the knowledge that, though the impulse may come from outside, the crucial response will be our own. Man's action makes a difference. And we know that it is perhaps this realization that makes possible the coming history that will, in Delany's sense, give birth to the new mythology.

Is such talk merely a diversion from our pressing political and religious preoccupation with the holding together of society? Or does it suggest that dissent is not nihilism but rather the prelude to the transformation of man—of the world—into something "different"? Again Delany has captured the fundamental suggestion which, while by no means conclusive, closes this study. Lobey addresses Spider:

> "The stories give you a law to follow—"
> "—that you can either break or obey."
> "They set you a goal—"
> "—and you can either fail that goal, succeed, or surpass it."
> "Why?" I demanded. "Why can't you just ignore the old stories? I'll go on [to] plumb the sea, find the Kid without your help. I can ignore those tales!"
> "You're living in the real world now," Spider said sadly. "It's come from something. It's going to something. Myths always lie in the most difficult places to ignore. They confound all family love and hate. You shy at them on entering or exiting any endeavor."
> [P. 120]

And again, in Spider's words:

> "Lobey, Earth, the world . . . the species that stands on two legs and roams this thin crust: it's changing, Lobey. It's not the same. Some people walk under the sun and accept that change, others close their eyes . . . that is how the humans acted throughout their history. We have taken over their abandoned world, and something new is happening to the fragments, something

we can't even define with mankind's leftover vocabulary. You must take its importance exactly as that: it is indefinable; you are involved in it; it is wonderful, fearful, deep, ineffable to your explanations, opaque to your efforts to see through it; yet it demands you take journeys, defines your stopping and starting points, can propel you with love and hate, even to seek death for Kid Death—"

"—or make me make music," I finished for him. "What are you talking about, Spider?" [P. 116]

notes

PREFACE

1. Jacques Ellul, "Between Chaos and Paralysis," *The Christian Century* (June 5, 1968), p. 750.
2. Samuel R. Delany, *The Einstein Intersection* (New York: Ace Books, 1967), p. 125.

CHAPTER 1.
Science Fiction—What Is It?

1. Jacob Brackman, *Esquire* (October 1968), p. 129.
2. Judith Merril, "Books," *The Magazine of Fantasy and Science Fiction* (November 1967).

CHAPTER 2.
The Tortured Journey of H. G. Wells

1. H. G. Wells, *After Democracy* (London: C. A. Watts & Co.).
2. Isaac Asimov, Introduction to *Two Novels by H. G. Wells: The Time Machine, The War of the Worlds* (New York: Fawcett Premier Books, 1968), p. 21.

CHAPTER 3.
Humanum: What Manner of Men Are We?

1. Frantz Fanon, *The Wretched of the Earth* (New York: Grove Press, 1963), pp. 253, 255.
2. A. E. van Vogt, *Slan* (New York: Simon & Schuster, 1951), p. 240.
3. A. E. van Vogt, *The Universe Maker* (New York: Ace Books, 1953), pp. 103-104.
4. Theodore Sturgeon, *More Than Human* (New York: Ballantine Books, 1953), p. 183.

5. Konrad Lorenz, *On Aggression*, trans. Marjorie Kerr Wilson (New York: Harcourt, Brace & World, 1966), ch. 14.
6. Robert A. Heinlein, *Stranger in a Strange Land* (New York: G. P. Putnam's Sons, 1961), p. 394.
7. Robert A. Heinlein, "Gulf," *Assignment in Eternity* (New York: Signet Books, 1953), pp. 42-43.
8. Cordwainer Smith, "The Dead Lady of Clown Town," *Space Lords* (New York: Pyramid Books, 1965), p. 101.
9. C. S. Lewis, *Out of the Silent Planet* (New York: The Macmillan Company, 1943), p. 150.
10. Fyodor Dostoevsky, "Notes from Underground," *The Short Novels of Dostoevsky* (New York: The Dial Press, 1945), p. 149.

CHAPTER 4.
Nature: Dynamism and Change

1. Lorenz, *On Aggression*, p. 229.
2. Arthur C. Clarke, *2001: A Space Odyssey* (New York: Signet Books, 1968), p. 185.
3. Hayden Howard, "Beyond Words," *The Magazine of Fantasy and Science Fiction* (July 1968), p. 125.
4. Thomas M. Disch, *echo round his bones* (New York: Berkley Medallion Books, 1967), p. 90.

CHAPTER 5.
History: Consciousness and the Fullness of Time

1. Walter M. Miller, Jr., *A Canticle for Leibowitz* (Philadelphia: J. B. Lippincott, 1959), p. 66.
2. Isaac Asimov, *Second Foundation* (New York: Avon Books, 1964), p. 91.
3. Isaac Asimov, *The End of Eternity* (New York: Signet Books, 1958), pp. 187-188.
4. Dostoevsky, "Notes from Underground," p. 152.
5. Aldous Huxley, *Brave New World* (New York: Harper & Row, 1946), pp. xvii-xx.
6. Herbert Butterfield, *Christianity and History* (New York: Charles Scribner's Sons, 1949, 1950), pp. 145-146.
7. J. G. Ballard, "The Cloud-Sculptors of Coral D," *The Magazine of Fantasy and Science Fiction* (December 1967), p. 120.
8. J. G. Ballard, *The Crystal World* (New York: Farrar, Straus & Giroux, 1966), pp. 95-96.

9. Robert Ardrey, *African Genesis* (New York: Dell Publishing Company, 1967), pp. 218-219.
10. J. G. Ballard, "The Screen Game," *The Impossible Man* (New York: Berkley Medallion Books, 1966), p. 71.
11. Ballard, "The Cloud-Sculptors of Coral D," p. 127.

CHAPTER 6.
The Shattered Ring:
Science Fiction and the Quest for Meaning

1. Roger Zelazny, *Lord of Light* (New York: Avon Books, 1967), p. 9.
2. Delany, *The Einstein Intersection*, p. 36.
3. Walter J. Ong, "Myth or Evolution? Crisis of the Creative Imagination," *McCormick Quarterly* (January 1965), p. 38.